CHURCHILL & ROOSEVELT
THE BIG SLEEPOVER
AT THE WHITE HOUSE

J. M. Wilson

CHURCHILL & ROOSEVELT
THE BIG SLEEPOVER
AT THE WHITE HOUSE

Christmas 1941-New Year 1942

James Mikel Wilson

Cover Design and Art Direction by Tod Gilpin

Proud Supporter:
National Churchill Museum and Fallen Warriors Memorial

gatekeeper press

Published by Gatekeeper Press
3971 Hoover Rd. Suite 77
Columbus, OH 43123-2839

Cover Design and Art Direction by Tod Gilpin, www.togilbrand.com

Editing by: David Aretha, Yellow Bird Editors

ISBN (paperback): 9781932549973
eISBN: 9781619849594

Printed in the United States of America

First Edition

READER PRAISE FOR THIS BOOK

"I really like the idea of focusing on those three weeks at the White House and on the relationship between Roosevelt and Churchill as a lens for the greater history lesson. It reminds me a bit of what the movie *Lincoln* did by focusing on Congress' vote to end slavery."

—Monte Francis, San Francisco
(author and four-time Emmy Award-winning journalist)

"The central theme of this book, the humanizing of these men as you place them in historical context, is incredibly moving. Also powerful, and what makes it stand out, is the way the conversations between the men range far and wide, giving context to so many connections I never knew existed."

—Matthew Arkin, California and New York
(author of *In the Country of the Blind* and American film, television, and theater actor and educator)

"I found myself reading it word by word, trying to absorb the importance of Churchill and Roosevelt's conversations and the effect they made on the next seventy years of my life. Both were leaders, both were actors and role players. Their mutual decisions have shaped the world we have lived in since that time."

—George Rootes, Houston
(Academy of Distinguished Alumni, University of Missouri)

"The two-person dialogue, in the first person, kept my attention, and some of the details were new to me. If this work also becomes a play, I can just picture Roosevelt sitting on stage in one of those old-time wheelchairs, and Churchill in a big overstuffed chair with his smoking jacket and cigar. Excellent job!"

—Charley Crew, San Diego
(past president, Rotary Club of Rancho Bernardo)

"So many things I didn't know about them. I found your book refreshing and very entertaining. I liked the approach of two monologues. I could just see them sitting by a fire reminiscing."

—Walter McDonald, Arlington Heights, Illinois
(president, The McDonald Group, Inc.)

"In the hands of the right artistic director, this also has the potential to be a brilliant play."

—Douglas Davis, Brooklyn (off-Broadway actor)

"I found your work delightful. It really did capture the two characters. I could almost hear them talking to me."

—Paul Wilkis, Delray Beach, Florida (history buff)

PROUD SUPPORTER

This book and the author are a Proud Supporter of the **Fallen Warriors Memorial** and America's **National Churchill Museum.** Both of these unique non-profit organizations would welcome your support too.

Fallen Warriors Memorial in Houston, Texas carries the names of the brave men and women who grew up in Texas, loved America with equal passion, and believed in protecting her shores from terrorism in Iraq, Afghanistan, and Globally. They gave their lives in Operation Iraqi Freedom, Operation New Dawn, and Operation Enduring Freedom so that we may enjoy our freedoms. We can never forget what they did for us, and the price they paid. This Memorial reminds us of their sacrifices and the families and friends who have suffered their loss. As of October 2015 634 names appear on the Memorial. To learn more go to www.fallenwarriorstexas.org

National Churchill Museum in Fulton, Missouri, on the campus of Westminster College, commemorates and celebrates the life, times, and distinguished career of Sir Winston Churchill and inspires visitors and future leaders by his example of resilience, determination, and resolution. In 2009 the Memorial received a congressional designation as America's National Churchill Museum.

At the invitation of President Harry Truman, Churchill delivered in 1946 one of his most significant speeches in his long and illustrious career on the Westminster campus. It was titled The Sinews of Peace and made the phrase "An Iron Curtain" part of the world's vocabulary. Throughout the year, the museum offers exhibits and educational material that reminds us that the more we look back in history, the further we can see ahead. The museum is housed beneath a Christopher Wren designed church that had stood in London since 1677. This magnificent building, badly damaged during World War II, was moved stone by stone to the college's campus and rebuilt to Wren's original specifications. To learn more go to www.nationalchurchillmuseum.org

CONTENTS

PREFACE

Churchill and Roosevelt: The Big Sleepover at the White House concentrates on a fateful three weeks that Winston Churchill and Franklin Roosevelt bonded and plotted under the same roof the demise of their common enemies. But it is more than a historical recitation of places and events. This book captures the human emotions, the strengths and frailties and individual agendas, sometimes conflicting, that the two men's personalities brought to the table.

Each character was an enormously complex person, fearless, persistent, visionary, and unwavering in his sense of time and place in history. If these two leaders had not engaged one another, forged a friendship, compromised, and united in a common cause, our lives might look very different today.

Even though both men were under enormous stress, they found time to laugh, philosophize, weep, and enjoy life's other pleasures.

As one reads this book, the author challenges the reader to look for parallels in our time . . . . What decisions did these two great men make that impact us yet today and what virtues did they possess that leaders now might emulate?

To make this work less like a history lesson, the author has chosen stylistically to present the story as a two-man monologue. This novel approach provides a useful way to become reacquainted with the principals. Each character alternatively reveals his thoughts about the other and each feeds off the other as their story unfolds. Although we may know the outcome, as the two men interface, they do not. As contradictory as it may seem, the author employs the present tense to give the storyline a sense of urgency and suspense.

Obviously not all the time Churchill and Roosevelt spent together has been completely documented. They had many private conversations while in Washington. Now seventy-five-plus years later, they have grown as historical as well as mythical figures.

Throughout the book, the logic of the situation sets the tone for the idea of the conversations Churchill and Roosevelt might have had. The author has taken the liberty of speculating about what they might have said to one another during some of their private moments.

The narrative is largely based on documentation such as events, dates, speeches, third parties, and places. What went on behind the view of the public eye is subject to conjecture . . . particularly their late evening escapades and aspects of their final farewell dinner. The author fleshes out the story by coloring it with conversations that might have occurred but that are not necessarily provable.

Lastly, the writer sets out to humanize these two epic leaders of their time and perhaps the century. He works to reveal not only their fears and tears but also their joys, humor, passions, temperaments, and schemes. He attempts to break into their minds and points of view as the two men join together intent on saving the Western world. So, this book may be called a work of creative nonfiction, with some elements of fiction and imagination woven into the plot to make the work more entertaining but no less relevant.

ACKNOWLEDGMENTS

The following individuals deserve acknowledgment for their significant time, effort, corrections, suggestions, and constructive and encouraging feedback to turn this germ of an idea into a small book.

Julian Lamborn, Sandra Lamborn, and Fred Mallett for their British perspectives and insights. The Lamborns can recall evacuation and bomb shelters. As a youngster, Fred remembers the aftermath of the war, with vacant sites and rubble. All three can remember the sound of Churchill's voice on the radio and image on news clips. Vic and Jerri Holy and Bob Madison, thank you for scrubbing the spelling and punctuation, a never-ending task. For their special encouragement: Pat and Colleen Hosford, Bob Wilkis, Paul Wilkis, Kevin Wilson, Warren Lee Smith, Charlie Crew, Monte Francis, Matthew Francis, Warren Lee Smith, George Rootes, Nancy Nollen, Douglas Davis, Tom Loiacano, and Katherine Wilson, my wife of forty-eight years, who knows how badly my creative work begs for editing! Johan Leach, Tom Loicano's mother-in-law and a member of the greatest generation, vividly recalls her war years in upstate New York, having worked for a company that manufactured weapons to support the war effort and staying tuned to FDR's fireside chats. After reading it three times herself, she was delighted to share the manuscript with colleagues in her senior living facility who remember well what they fought for.

A thank you goes to Barry Singer, owner of Chartwell Booksellers in Manhattan and author of *Churchill Style*. He confirmed that to the best of his knowledge a book in this format about Churchill and Roosevelt has never been written.

And for his historical perspective, I would like to thank Dr. William

Urban, Lee L. Morgan Professor of History and International Studies, Monmouth College. His insights and guidance reshaped aspects of the manuscript, along with reassurances that the work captures much of the essence of Churchill and Roosevelt's personalities and exchanges.

Also Matthew Arkin deserves my gratitude for his professional critique, as does my editor, David Aretha, for his sharp pencil, direction, and guidance. They profoundly affected the final product.

A reminder, *Churchill and Roosevelt: The Big Sleepover at the White House* draws upon historical facts and events and then merges them with a fictional account of what might have been said during their time together.

BOOK COVERS AND TITLE PAGE

On the front cover, the extraordinary *Allies* sculpture by Lawrence Holofcener depicts Winston Churchill and Franklin Roosevelt chatting on a park bench. This particular life size work is from a private collection, image courtesy of Bonhams British Auction House. My gratitude to Mr. and Mrs. Holofcener for their approval too. *Allies* will endure long after these pages are forgotten however similar objectives may have been to honor Churchill and Roosevelt. To learn more about Mr. Holofcener's remarkable career and wide ranging artistic contributions visit www.holofcener.com

On the title page, the absolutely perfect cartoon of Franklin Roosevelt and Winston Churchill in their pajamas leaning out of the White House bedroom windows was drawn in December 1941 by Clifford Berryman, staff cartoonist for the *Washington Star*. Mr. Berryman (1869-1949) was a prolific political cartoonist and even drew cartoons of Franklin's cousin, Teddy Roosevelt.

On the back cover, Glyn Lowe shot the photo of the South Portico of the White House decked out for Christmas. For similar striking images and to appreciate Mr. Lowe's immense talents, visit his gallery at Life At Shutter Speed, Glyn Lowe Photoworks, www.glynlowe.com

Tod Gilpin did the wonderful design work and art direction on the front and back covers as well as my previous book, *Paw Tracks Here and Abroad: A dog's Tale*. To learn more about his many amazing talents, and to see his striking artistic and professional work, visit www.togilbrand.com

DEDICATION

This book is dedicated to "The Greatest Generation," including my father, Captain Swisher Wilson, U.S. Army, and my uncles, Captain Jim Baird, U.S. Navy; Birl Wilson, FBI; Mike Wilson, Intelligence Corps; Lyle Wilson and Herb Smith, Iowa farmers, and Nat Baird, high school coach and teacher. It is also dedicated to all the women and men across America who sacrificed at home and abroad to preserve freedom. Captain Baird served as a gunnery officer on December 7, 1941, on board the USS *Helena* at Pearl Harbor. The Japanese finally sank his ship at the Battle of Kula Gulf on July 5, 1943 . . . but not without one hell of a fight! Birl helped hunt down enemy spies on U.S. soil. Swish served in Detroit, developing service and operation manuals for military vehicles. Lyle and Herb fed a hungry nation and its allies at war. Nat instilled values and knowledge to help his students become responsible citizens in their communities.

Introduction

SETTING THE STAGE

In December 1941, the Western world dangled by a thread, with the voracious Nazi Germany and Imperial Japan wolves eager to devour it. While British, Russian, and fragmented resistance forces fought bravely and valiantly, their resources were steadily being exhausted, though not their will. They needed a Herculean partner. Winston Churchill prayed that perhaps the United States, although ill equipped at that time for global warfare, might take up arms and help deliver salvation.

This desperate era and the Allies' sense of urgency under assault seem remote for most of us today. Relatively few survivors remain, and for the rest of us the lessons are frozen in history books. How can we gain a sense of the emotion and begin to fathom the desperation and dark days of those times?

To give the reader a more contemporary perspective, we can look today at the brutal actions inflicted by the Islamic State in Iraq and Syria (ISIS), or just a few decades back to the murderous forces of Pol Pot in Cambodia. Although ISIS' actions are more regionalized, parallels exist between their brutality and the Imperial Japanese and Nazi leaders' thuggery. ISIS' brutal tactics to terrorize people into submission, land grabs in the name of Allah, distorted and archaic religious beliefs, enslavement of people, execution of ethnic groups, and manipulation of poorly educated and/or unemployed youth strike a familiar ring. So does the slaughter by Boko Haram in Nigeria and neighboring countries.

Fortunately, history proves that terroristic, disruptive, raw force does not prevail in an enlightened, educated world. It violates the fundamental nature and goodness of man, which eventually rises up to resist suppressed freedoms and brutal totalitarianism.

Over the Christmas holiday of 1941, British Prime Minister Winston Churchill and U.S. President Franklin Roosevelt met for almost three weeks to plan the defeat of Germany and Japan. They came away with a Christmas gift for the American and British peoples—a promise of deliverance from the flames of World War II.

Shortly after Japan bombed Pearl Harbor on December 7, Churchill suggested a visit. Initially, Roosevelt tried to dissuade him from coming, both for political reasons and because a voyage across the Atlantic Ocean practically invited attack by German submarines.

However, since Hitler and Mussolini had immediately declared war on the United States, this gave the two leaders of the English-speaking world common enemies. Moreover, the issues to be discussed could not await the slow process of diplomacy and formal notes. Effective transatlantic phone service was more than a decade away. Therefore, Churchill's journey and visit as Roosevelt's guest in the White House was arranged, but with extraordinary caution, secrecy, and boldness.

Possessing the confidence, skill, and power to alter events, both men exhibited dominant and strong-willed personalities. They were as likely to butt heads as get along.

Roosevelt advocated a liberal viewpoint and Churchill a conservative one. Churchill still believed in paternal colonialism and was reluctant to surrender any portion of the British Empire. Roosevelt sought to end imperial dominance. Churchill was a detailed-oriented, put-it-in-writing and document-it kind of person. Roosevelt was a big-picture guy who didn't particularly care for putting things down precisely on paper. They would eventually discover how badly they needed one another and forge a bond of brotherhood.

As a White House guest, Churchill spent almost three weeks during his sojourn getting to know Roosevelt on an intensely personal basis. No other head of state has ever spent so much time in the White House before or since his visit. While living there, Churchill's spirit enveloped the White House, its occupants, and its visitors—so much so that the author chose the word *occupation* to describe one of the chapters in the book.

While together, the two men began to establish a spirit of cooperation and more importantly trust. It would prevail through the remainder of the war and ultimately lead to victory. One can only imagine and speculate on the lively and pivotal conversations that transpired between these two great characters, leaders of their generation.

The book strives to strike a balance between educating and entertaining the reader about events and likely exchanges that occurred between these marvelous men who were cast in their roles by circumstance, preparation, and privilege. The narrative reflects their character, humor, strength, frailties, and fears as they courageously led their respective nations through the darkest of days in the twentieth century.

Both men came from well-respected, influential families . . . born to privileges that the average man on the street could not begin to comprehend. Ironically, as boys they loved many of the same children's stories and rhymes. They were both enthralled by naval heroics and stories at sea and liked being near the water. Military strategy held their interest and they played with toy soldiers while envisioning great conquests. After these parallel interests, their upbringing diverged, and it shaped the qualities that eventually enriched their friendship.

Churchill's parents, even by English upper-class customs, provided him little succorance. His father, Lord Randolph Churchill, was preoccupied with politics and money matters most of his life. He treated Winston coldly, almost like he was a nuisance in the household, and was inclined to belittle rather than nourish him . . . if he paid any attention to him at all!

In later years he would describe his American mother Jennie with sad reverence. She was a glamorous high society lady who delegated much of the child-rearing chores to fortunately a compassionate, loving nanny. But Winston worshipped Jennie even though she shined like a remote star and always remained grateful to his nanny. It's amazing his parents' aloofness didn't cripple his spirit, ambition, and will to succeed.

Perhaps because he was so ignored as a little one, Winston always had a tendency to seek approval from those he respected. He sometimes exhibited other childlike behaviors, which amazingly served him well. While the private schools of his time encouraged suppression of feelings while maintaining a stiff upper lip, Winston was in touch with his feelings. He could articulate his emotions in a unique way to influence others, as evidenced in portions of three speaches included in this work. He wore his sentiments on his sleeve and could shed tears without embarrassment. He was never reluctant to seek forgiveness when he was wrong or remain angry at those who apologized for whatever grievance.

Unlike Churchill's parents, Roosevelt's visibly loved and nourished him. He was the only child of a fifty-three-year-old father and an admiring twenty-seven-year-old mother determined to give him every opportunity to excel. In such an environment, Roosevelt grew secure, confidant, and intellectually above average. Using these assets to his advantage, he learned early in life how to affect others and even maneuver them to his point of view.

At age thirty-nine, Roosevelt fell victim to polio, and he would be confined to a wheelchair for the rest of his life. As president, he drew upon his enormous skills to manipulate others, sometimes deviously, to offset perceptions that he was extremely crippled. At the time, the American people perceived handicaps in their leaders as a sign of potential weakness.

Roosevelt and Churchill's complementary yet contrasting personalities set the stage for this work, as does their rapidly evolving friendship. Both men had a keener sense than average of their roles in history, and it enhanced their relationship. Look for similarities, as well as their differences, in a few of their speeches that are included in the story line.

History views Roosevelt as the better politician, more circumspect by nature, and Churchill the more transparent and warmer human being.

Churchill had already spent a couple of years struggling against tyranny. He'd been to many dark places. His emotions and personal sense of compassion, as well as an engaging leadership style forged from the experience, was quite evident in his speeches. On the other hand, Roosevelt could only anticipate what was about to happen to his country and, as a result, was just a bit more mechanical in expressing himself, but no less effective.

Astutely aware of their times, Roosevelt and Churchill were master communicators and branders of their personas. They effectively sought out and used press conferences to tell their political stories to their constituents. In leading and inspiring their nations, both understood the power of mass media and how to manipulate them . . . newsreels, photographs, radio, newspapers, and magazines. They also effectively used props to their advantage.

For example, Roosevelt often posed for the camera with his long, powerful jaw and chin protruding upwards, and his lips and teeth clinching a Camel cigarette in its ivory holder on the same sprightly angle. Added to this image of public confidence was his loyal, always present dog Fala by his side or perched on his lap. Similarly staged to affect his British citizens, Churchill was often photographed holding an eight-inch Cuban Romeo y Julieta cigar in his hand and his jaw clinched in defiance of his enemies, as well as a cane by his side to beat off tyranny.

Throughout the Great Depression, Roosevelt remained confident in the future in store for America. He sustained that same optimism throughout the war, and this aspect of his strong personality constituted his genius as a forceful and creative president and leader.

In contrast, Churchill was so immersed in Britain's day-to-day struggle to resist the pounding from the Axis powers that he found little time or energy to contemplate the future beyond the current inferno. If anything, he wished to push through the war and successfully preserve Britain's imperial greatness and role in world affairs. However, he adamantly feared and opposed socialism and remained paranoid about Russia and its appetite to enfold other countries under communistic rule.

In an unusual format, this book plays out more as a two-man monologue than a dialogue, with Winston and Franklin reflecting and interacting on the time spent with the other during this exceptional occurrence in our nation's history. While the book is founded on facts and history, the author exercises great liberty in imagining Winston and Franklin's discussions and presenting the special chemistry evolving between these two men as they engage one another. The conversational monologue gives the story a unique flavor.

The Big Sleepover is entirely chronological, which is the best way to tell the story because the most interesting aspect is the chronology . . . the order in which things happen. Although the reader may know how events occurred, the characters do not until they happen. The story reveals their desires, fears, sorrows, anger, frustrations, ambitions, gamesmanship, humor, and joy.

There are contemporary lessons applicable yet today from the courage these two men exhibited to advance their beliefs, compromise where necessary, lead their nations, and offer a vision of a new world order. Many of the decisions they made still affect our lives, from the creation of a United Nations to the dismantling of imperialism and the redrawing of international boundaries.

In character, here are Winston and Franklin.

Chapter One

A CLANDESTINE RENDEZVOUS

January 20-February 9, 1941

Roosevelt

Early in the war, I asked Churchill to keep me personally informed of events unfolding in Europe. He understands the existing limitations on me for direct U.S. involvement. We frequently exchange confidential communications, sealed in diplomatic pouches and delivered by courier. Last month he sent me a desperate letter saying that Britain is running out of cash to pay for war provisions and that they urgently need any kind of help we might offer. However, he does not specify exactly what help they need.

Through these communications, I have come to identify with his plight, unusual optimism, and extreme courage. He is the last lion standing between Hitler and the rest of the civilized world. Through it all, he exemplifies amazing leadership, heroism, humor, and grace. I am actually beginning to respect and admire the man, aside from his stand on ceremony and advocacy of British imperialism around the world.

But, after much of Western Europe surrendered to the Nazis, two big concerns bother me. First, does Great Britain possess the resources to continue to resist? Secondly, does Churchill have the resolve to carry on the fight?

To find out, in January I decide to send my most trusted friend and confidant, Harry Hopkins, to London to meet personally with

Churchill to assess these issues. I know Harry's personal reservations about meeting with Churchill. He doesn't particularly like Churchill's aristocratic behavior nor share his conservative beliefs. But I know that I can depend on Harry's objectivity and, besides, at the moment I am unable to travel. Also, Harry will insulate me from making any hasty decisions that might have repercussions with Congress.

Churchill

A few weeks ago, I got a telegram from Roosevelt informing me that he is sending an emissary from Washington, Harry Hopkins, to spend two weeks meeting with me and other leaders both in government and industry. He also wishes to visit sites devastated by German bombers and talk to people on the street and in shops to personally assess our situation. He knows that the war has been going poorly for us, with one defeat after another. Since U.S. Ambassador Joseph Kennedy left his post in October of last year, there has been no Executive Office presence in London to build a relationship with. But honestly we don't miss Kennedy.

I of course diplomatically consent to the visit, but immediately harbor personal reservations. Yes, I am eager at every opportunity to improve our ties to the U.S. and beg for supplies that we desperately need to continue the fight. I would like nothing more for the U.S. to jump into the war. Yet, I am apprehensive about meeting a complete stranger.

Who is Harry Hopkins? Clearly meeting with him could prove a pivotal event for us. There could be a lot at stake here. I make further inquiries and learn that the man I am about to meet currently holds no official title. Evidently, he lives and works in the White House. I think to myself, perhaps this man called Harry has been masquerading as a janitor? Of course not!

I also learned that he was born in Sioux City, Iowa, and I think that's somewhere in the Midwest, perhaps what was once Indian country. My researchers say Hopkins also went to Grinnell College in Iowa and oddly enough, while there, took perhaps the first political science course ever offered in the United States. I muse that perhaps the college garnered such expertise negotiating treaties with the local Indian tribes.

I am informed that after college, Hopkins rose in the ranks of the Red Cross and then parlayed his leadership and organizational skills acquired there to head up Roosevelt's Works Progress Administration, employing millions of people off the streets during the Depression. In 1938 he became secretary of commerce and continued to play a strong role in helping drive the country's recovery until he resigned from that position last year. While a cabinet member he and Roosevelt became close friends, and it is rumored that Hopkins is one of the very few people who can read the president's inner thoughts.

From what I now know about Hopkins, I remain hopeful that a meeting with him will prove fruitful, but of course I am an optimist at heart.

Roosevelt

After meeting with Harry to discuss his pending trip to London, I am sitting alone at my desk in the Oval Office fiddling. Surrounded by knickknacks meaningful only to me and my stamp collection affectionately cluttering my desk, I reflect back on the events that have been unfolding in Europe.

I personally view the Nazi threat as far greater than a quarrel among neighboring countries. I sense that even if we remain insulated and isolated from the battles raging in Europe, eventually our next generation of young Americans will be sucked into fighting that regime's appetite for world dominion. And, if we lose that conflict, it could be years, if not several generations, before democracy, as we cherish it, could ever be restored.

But quite frankly, our polls showed that 80 percent of U.S. citizens view the conflagration as mainly a spat among European states.

Even our own ambassador to Great Britain, and my former friend and political ally, Joseph Kennedy, has discouraged U.S. involvement. Now I am furious with him. After the Germans trapped most of the British troops in France on the beach in Dunkirk, Kennedy coldly remarked that he candidly believed "Britain was down the tube" and that democracy would end there.

Our families had once been very close but now I don't give a damn that Kennedy and my son James had been business partners. I'd find something else to drink! After Prohibition ended in 1933, my son and Kennedy made a trip to Scotland to acquire distribution rights for

Scotch whiskey. The resulting company, Somerset Importers, became the exclusive supplier for not only Dewar's Scotch Whiskey but also Gordon's Gin.

For his ill-timed and embarrassing remark, I quietly but forcefully orchestrated Kennedy's resignation in November 1940. I plan to replace him with John Winant, three-time governor of New Hampshire. I expect that John will do a great job repairing diplomatic relations and quickly befriend Churchill and King George VI. But, until I can get him relocated to London, Harry will provide the conduit of information I need to know to decide whether to try harder to escalate our support of Britain's war efforts.

Charles Lindbergh, the first man to fly solo across the Atlantic, equally opposes U.S. intervention. In the case of Lindbergh, a technocrat himself, he sincerely believes the Germans possess superior technology and cannot be beaten. His strong views make him "the unofficial leader and spokesman for America's isolationists." I will never forgive him for the pain and aggravation his stance causes. Not since the Civil War has our nation been so divided over an issue. I think to myself, rather vindictively, that if we should ever go to war, I will refuse Lindbergh, as famous as he is, an air force commission . . . should he have the nerve to request one.

We also have a fairly large German and Irish population who are politically biased against the U.S. going to war in Europe. One can only surmise their motives. Rumors abound that the Nazis have promised the Irish independence should they acquiesce in defeating England.

Worse yet, the FBI and other intelligence services inform me that Nazi agents have been slipping money to senators and others to try to persuade me to push Churchill into making peace with Hitler.

In general, Americans don't believe that Europeans share much in common with them. They haven't traveled abroad and communicate infrequently, if at all, with relatives there. The average American views the raging war kind of like a movie—something that just doesn't have a real or immediate effect on their lives.

Plus, many of our older citizens harbor bad memories of World War I. We lost fifty thousand lives in a war that they don't believe benefited the United States—especially after the whole thing seemed to be repeating itself with the resurgence of the Nazis' military machine.

Our students in particular voice their opposition. They know they will be the ones going into battle for a cause that they yet understand or support. At Yale, students have created the Americans First movement, which has quickly spread to other college campuses. Some members against U.S. intervention in the war include the sons of prominent and influential families, the likes of Gerald Ford, John F. Kennedy, Potter Stewart, Sargent Shriver, Kingman Brewster, and Kurt Vonnegut. None of them want to get a draft letter or a phone call from their dear old Uncle Sam!

As if to put an exclamation point on our current political differences, a recent harsh debate between isolationist and interventionist congressmen ended in an undignified pugilistic brawl on the floor of the House. I secretly hoped that the interventionists threw a few good punches. But most of our congressmen have long since outgrown their fighting weight.

To make matters worse, we are not on any kind of war footing. In 1940 Nazi Germany had roughly five million men in arms when we had a paltry 280,000 regular soldiers and a like number in the National Guard.

The best I can do under these conditions, without destroying my own political career, is to play for time. After visiting Churchill, I hope that Hopkins may be able to give me the ammunition I need to do this.

Churchill

Harry Hopkins has arrived in London. We are an odd match and both realize it after our first couple of days together. I am almost old enough to be Harry's father, so not only do we have generational differences to surmount, we come from different political bents. It doesn't take me long to realize that he is what we would call a progressive social worker and reformer. But, I like him. By our British standards, he is plain-speaking, bright, and disarmingly and casually informal. Music to my ears, he says he is here to listen. Ha! I wonder if he has heard how much I like listeners.

So, over a three-and-a-half-hour lunch at No. 10 Downing Street beside a crackling fireplace, I take the opportunity to recap events that began to unfold on Friday, September 1, 1939. This was the day that the sinisterly mustached, detestable "bastard" Adolf Hitler invaded Poland.

I tell Harry that upon learning of the invasion, I quietly told my beloved wife Clemmie that if "Hitler invaded Hell, I would make a favorable reference to the devil in the House of Commons!" He listens intently and says he would love to meet Clementine.

I explain to Harry that I had quarreled repeatedly with Prime Minister Neville Chamberlain. He appeased Hitler. He let too many opportunities slip by to demonstrate the British Lion's stiffer spine toward Hitler's hoodlum and bullying behavior.

I ask, "Harry, do you know the definition of an appeaser?" He says, "No." And I continue. "He is one who feeds a crocodile, hoping it will eat him last!" Chamberlain refused to apply tough diplomatic pressure to fight for what was right when we could easily have won without bloodshed. Now the crocodile feeds savagely on Europe!

I knew that Britain could no longer sit passively by and tolerate Germany's invasion of Poland and, eventually, the rest of Eastern Europe.

So, on September 3, an infamous Sunday morning, matters finally became clearer.

Poorly equipped to confront a bully, we bravely and proudly declared war on Germany. And, Chamberlain promptly appointed me first lord of the Admiralty, a job I held previously during World War I. It was just the forum I needed to maneuver him to retirement.

Now that the vultures had come home to roost throughout Europe, I wanted Chamberlain's job. Eventually I got it when he was forced by the House of Commons to resign in May 1940. But, be careful what you wish for! It comes with burdens.

After his embarrassing defeat, I set aside our animosities and invited Chamberlain to become a member of our War Cabinet to help unite his party to our common cause.

Of course, Harry knows that by June 1940, Germany's superior preparation for war and military tactics led to the collapse of France, along with other nations. With new, vastly superior armaments and mobility never seen before in the history of warfare, the Germans have accomplished in eleven days what they had failed to do in four years of bitter fighting in World War I. Harry registers his respect for Britain's resolve under such seemingly insurmountable disadvantages.

I explain that our king and Parliament were not disillusioned. We realized that as the only ones standing between Hitler and his absolute domination of Western Europe, this effectively made us military orphans. We knew we would soon need to confront the reality of an eventual German invasion.

If we surrendered, we recognized we would be living in a hellish existence anyway. So, rather than capitulate like those countries already there, Britain decided to plunge through hell and try its best to make it through to the other side.

Then, I throw him my best pitch. I say, "Harry, if your country gives us the tools and materials to continue to fight, please assure President Roosevelt we will do our duty to defend the free world, alone if necessary."

Roosevelt

I am getting progressively encouraging dispatches from Hopkins. With the exception of meeting key members of Parliament, the cabinet, and some military and industrial leaders, he has been meeting almost exclusively and privately with Churchill for more than four weeks, far more than the two intended. This trip will for certain blow the travel budget! He has spent weekends at Chequers, the Prime Minister's estate, and gotten to know his wife, Clementine, and his daughters. Harry is a great storyteller and I sense that between hours of smoking cigars and cigarettes and consuming Scotch, he has gotten beyond Churchill's veneer and shrewdly assessed the British fighting spirit.

Hopkins' insights have accomplished in a few weeks what Ambassador Kennedy had been unable to see, hear, or wanted to report. His input just reinforces my decision to send a new ambassador to London. I also realize, given Hopkins' formidable skills as a communicator and facilitator, that more than likely the White House now will have a sub-rosa ambassador living in the White House with me . . . one who can bridge communications between Churchill and me.

The last night before he leaves, I get one last telegram from Hopkins. It reads: "Mr. President, this island needs our immediate assistance with everything we can get them."

Churchill

Even Clemmie, who often criticizes my political colleagues and late-night carousing friends, really seems to like Hopkins. She has observed how comfortable he is to have around Chequers, our historical country retreat for prime ministers to entertain dignitaries and guests.

My wife enjoys him teasing me . . . especially about my own paintings, which are liberally displayed hither and thither throughout the house. I find painting landscapes thoroughly relaxing and, unlike politics, if you make a mistake, you simply paint over it. Hopkins agrees and then suggests that I have perhaps an even brighter career ahead of me as an artist, and the sooner we get this damn war over, the faster I can get back to my true calling of splashing paint on canvass. Semi-seriously, he wants my first painting after the war to be a portrait of him and me toasting victory to one another on the front steps of No. 10 Downing Street.

We have become friends and my instincts now say to trust Hopkins to the core. It doesn't hurt our relationship that he is an inveterate night owl like myself and enjoys pre-bedtime libations to help lullaby oneself to sleep.

Hopkins has been here almost six weeks. On his last evening in Britain, several members of my cabinet and I host a special dinner for Hopkins. He brings me to tears when he reads a personal note from Roosevelt.

It is from the Book of Ruth: "Thy people shall be my people and thy God, my God, even to the end."

I think I know what this message means. Suddenly, I feel the joy of a drowning man who has just been thrown a lifeline.

After dinner, Hopkins tells me privately that he intends to recommend to Roosevelt that they do everything possible to help us, short of joining the war. But ever cautious not to get in front of his headlights given the divisive political situation in America, he adds that he cannot guarantee how soon or in what form that aid may come. He also strongly suggests that Roosevelt and I meet personally sometime over the next six months.

While Hopkins has been traveling throughout Britain to learn more about our wartime needs from civilian, military, and political leaders, Wendell Willkie also calls on me in London to present a personal letter from Roosevelt.

Last November Willkie ran against Roosevelt on the conservative ticket and lost the election. With apprehension, I observed the bitter campaign between the foes. Willkie ran on a conservative, isolationist platform. Had he won, it would have made the probability of any help from the United States even more unlikely . . . at least in the short term.

The fact that Willkie has come to see me so soon after losing the election suggests an amazing transformation. Even he finally subscribes to Roosevelt's campaign rhetoric! By knocking on my door, Willkie's visit symbolizes that some of America's extreme isolationists are beginning to soften their views. With a smile on his face, Willkie hands me Roosevelt's letter and patiently waits for me to open it. I am very touched. The letter recites a Longfellow poem that moves me to tears:

> *Sail on ship of state.*
> *Sail on union strong and great.*
> *Humanity with all its fears*
> *Is hanging breathless on thy fate.*

In a radio speech shortly afterward, I proudly mention Roosevelt's letter as a symbol of the emerging Anglo-American partnership. Both Hopkins and Willkie's visit during the first month of Roosevelt's new term gives our citizens encouragement that we live firmly in the prayers and thoughts of another great nation.

July 13-August 4, 1941

Roosevelt

Following Hopkins' January meeting with Churchill and his cabinet, he continues to provide me the intelligence and impetus to campaign harder to help Britain.

At Churchill's strong urging, I agreed to meet in May with British Rear Admiral John Godfrey, director of Royal Navy Intelligence, and his aide, Lieutenant Commander Ian Fleming, in the Oval Office. At Churchill's directive, they implored me to create a modern intelligence network to ferret out potential enemy activities. I listened intently to their rationale and quickly agreed that such a move might prove in the best interest of the United States. It certainly was worth further exploration. Until now, we really had not given the matter much consideration, content to let eight different agencies gather and handle foreign intelligence as an ancillary activity. None of them coordinated or shared much information with one another, and following WWI we had let this function atrophy, particularly in the shadow of the Depression years. Our lethargy on the matter had led us to an attitude of who would want to spy on a nation with millions of people out of work and practically a zero defense budget? Some threat!

Our military leaders and many in Congress, who would otherwise be sympathetic, take the view that protecting the home front comes first. They fear that whatever we send to Britain will make one less resource available to America. And, if we began to fulfill the avalanche of war supplies Churchill requests, my countrymen worry: What if he surrenders anyway? Will our potential enemies confiscate the aid we've sent and use it against us? I must somehow overcome these legitimate yet overly cautionary concerns.

Our most right wing conservatives take the view that we should simply let the Nazis and communist Russia destroy one another. These folks are too entrenched in their hardcore beliefs for me to waste my energy in trying to enlighten them.

Throughout the first half of this year, with increasing apprehension, I have been following the collapse of France and Eastern Europe and the mounting British losses at sea and on land. Germany's General Erwin Rommel, known as the "Desert Fox" for his skill and cunning, dominated the North African desert with his legion of tanks. In the face of mounting air raids on England, the British maintain their resolve to carry on alone. Even their victories carry huge losses.

In May 1941, the sinking of Germany's *Bismarck*, the newest and most powerful battleship in the world, also resulted in the destruction of the *Hood*, the largest and fastest British battleship. The *Hood* sank with a loss of fifteen hundred lives. I say a prayer for these British sailors and think to myself we must act quickly to help salvage the situation in Europe and Eastern Europe.

Since Hopkins' initial visit with Churchill, I have been devoting most of my energies to working behind the scenes to support our British friends. Through good old-fashioned execution of presidential power and backdoor politics and political favor, I manage to get the U.S. Neutrality Act amended under the new Lend Lease Act. This action now allows the sale of arms to belligerents on a cash and carry basis. But, they must take delivery in the U.S.

Theoretically, the definition of belligerents could apply to both the Germans and the British. However, I have used the power of my office on behalf of only one country. Our first act under the Lend Lease bill will provide Britain fifty surplus American destroyers to replace many of their vessels that the Germans sunk. Churchill will like the terms: ninety-nine years free rent!

By rearming Britain and its allies, I believe we will accomplish several things that will help convince my military and political colleagues to endorse the plan. First, it will buy time for us to change the views of the American people toward events in Europe. As a nation, we are still coming out of a depression. Manufacturing and sales of armaments creates badly needed jobs for our people. It also begins to set the foundation to build a robust military defense industry capable of supporting our American citizens should they be called upon to go to war.

I am now also totally convinced that we really ought to aid not only Britain but also Russia. We are already supporting China's efforts to stall Japan's invasion of their homeland. I send Hopkins back to London to inform Churchill and his cabinet of our decisions. Then, I ask him to continue onward to Moscow to determine exactly what kind of munitions and materials the Russians need. Also, Hopkins knows that I hope to head off any imperial aims and side agreements that I suspect Churchill might try to cut with Stalin, in the absence of our involvement. I grant him plenipotentiary powers to persuade Stalin to join our camp.

Churchill

For the second time in the last six months, Hopkins comes to London. Despite his assurances, we have seen very little in the ways of specific actions since Hopkins' visit in January and our conditions have further deteriorated under the Nazis' relentless nighttime bombings over London and elsewhere across the country. My cabinet and I joyfully greet him, anxious to learn if any of the assistance we requested—actually begged for—would be forthcoming.

Hopkins seems haggard from the trip. He appears even thinner than when I last saw him. His clothes cling limply to his small, shrunken frame. He looks like a Sad Sack cartoon character, with a limp cigarette hanging out of the corner of his lips. But there's nothing soft about this man, and anytime he opens his mouth we have learned from his last visit to listen with admiration. He possesses an extraordinary talent for putting complicated issues into perspective, and then—in very plain, homespun English—offer elegant and quite creative solutions. He remains absolutely loyal to his boss and has no airs or pretensions. I appreciate that he has been my voice in the White House over the past several months.

Hopkins brings us celebratory news! He says that the U.S. is putting a plan in motion to provide us military equipment and ships, munitions, food, and hospital supplies. Since Germany invaded them in June, we have been providing the Russians as much as we could spare, which unfortunately is very little. The meager effort has further depleted our supplies.

Germany's surprise invasion caught Joseph Stalin off guard. He thought he had a neutrality agreement with Hitler. With military swiftness and particular brutality, the Nazis virtually destroyed Russia's air force and captured several hundred thousand troops, many of whom were quickly executed.

Quite frankly, Hitler's decision to shift military resources to invade Russia gives some temporary relief for Britain. But if the Germans defeat Russia, we will soon feel again the full brunt of their armed forces and renewed air strikes on Britain. Therefore, I think it prudent to offer Stalin our full support as well as an alliance.

After informing us of America's plans to step up aid, Hopkins tells me he intends to rest for a few days and then immediately fly from London to Russia to explore Stalin's receptivity to a three-way alliance should America be drawn into the war. Although he doesn't say so directly, Hopkins alludes to America's position that it does not want any kind of agreement between Russian and Britain to take place without having some of their own strategic interests protected. He also believes that he can bring Stalin into our camp with a similar offer of material and munitions.

We both agree that Russia's situation is fragile with the loss of its air force and already so many soldiers. We must do whatever we can to keep Russia in the fight. At all costs we must stop Germany from acquiring

Russia's tremendous reserves of oil and other raw materials and prevent them from turning the Russian people into slave laborers.

When Hopkins leaves for Russia, at his suggestion, I call President Roosevelt to thank him for his military aid and to set in motion a clandestine meeting with me on August 9, 1941, in Placentia Bay. This is a rocky inlet on the south coast of Newfoundland, whose shore over the years has supported a tiny commercial fishing settlement. To my delight he accepts.

Roosevelt

After meeting with Stalin for only two days and imprudently consuming a fountain of Vodka to help lubricate their intensive conversations, Hopkins returns to London encouraged but absolutely ill and exhausted from such a demanding trip. He telegrams me that he now has a clearer understanding of Russia's situation. He comes away from the sessions impressed by Stalin's blunt speaking resolve—expressed in very salty language—to defeat Germany at any cost. He says, "Details to follow when we next meet."

Churchill sends me a telegram that his personal doctor has ordered a blood transfusion and extended bed rest for Harry to help restore his stamina. He's apparently quite anemic. His flight to Russia was brutal, taking over twenty hours nonstop on a Catalina airboat seated in a chilly unheated cabin. The return trip was even worse. I think to myself that Stalin can't help but admire Hopkins' toughness and grittiness to negotiate an alliance under such circumstances.

Churchill

Since Hopkins has proved so valuable a go-between among Roosevelt, myself, and now Stalin, I offer him passage back to North America with me on the expedition to meet Roosevelt in Newfoundland. He gladly accepts rather than risk another tortuous flight on an airboat hop-skipping across the Atlantic. I figure he might get some badly needed rest during the voyage, under the continued care of my personal physician. But, my act of kindness is not all for charity.

I want to seize this opportunity to continue to forge a positive and influential relationship with Hopkins since he is virtually connected at the hip with Roosevelt and will of course participate in our rendezvous. And it's no secret that I immensely enjoy his satirical sense of humor and quick mind . . . even if he is a socialistic liberal do-gooder. I might add a damn fine one.

Even I, an ardent conservative, recognize that after the war Britain may need to implement the kind of programs Hopkins put in place over the last six years. This may necessitate some form of social security and works programs. Such funding would employ large numbers of returning soldiers to help rebuild badly decaying and destroyed infrastructure. But I can't focus on these matters now. We have a war to win.

During the voyage, in addition to what I have already read and the intelligence received from our embassy personnel in America, I hope to learn more from Hopkins about Roosevelt's background, beliefs, and values as well as his accomplishments as a politician and leader. I must go to school on Roosevelt while in Hopkins' company. I am working against the hourglass and must count every tumbling grain of sand as an opportunity that might give me a better understanding of which hot buttons to press with Roosevelt.

August 9-11, 1941

Roosevelt

So when Churchill invited me a couple of weeks ago to meet him in Newfoundland, I readily agreed to the rendezvous. In addition to my two sons, Franklin Jr. and Elliott, I decide to take only a small group of our most senior military commanders. They include Generals George Marshall and Henry "Hap" Arnold and Admirals Ernest King and Harold Stark.

To avoid a congressional uproar, I camouflage this outing in the utmost secrecy. I tell Eleanor and the White House staff that I need a few days off the job and plan to take the boys on a long overdue fishing trip up the New England coast on the *Potomac*, my presidential yacht and floating White House.

Bless my dear discrete and sensitive wife. She doesn't believe me, of course, but she plays along with my little chicanery. She knows me well enough not to ask questions when I volunteer no further information.

To fool the press I leave a look-alike on board the *Potomac* who appears to be trolling for fish with a group of colleagues. Once far enough off shore so as not to be seen, I complete a secretive transfer to a heavy cruiser, the USS *Augusta*, the flagship of our Atlantic fleet. The game of charades is on.

Ha! Now, the *Augusta* is a world-class fishing boat extraordinaire . . . capable of blasting and depth charging the biggest of fish out of the water—totally filleted, no less, on the way down!

But, I am on a different kind of "fishing trip." I angle for our senior military leaders to get to know for the first time some of their British counterparts. I have been sensing that it is just a matter of time before our souring diplomatic relationships with Germany will totally collapse. Will it be in one year or three? I just don't know.

On the cruise up to Newfoundland I think back on what I know about Churchill and how best to engage the man, as well as provide him encouragement. Along the way, I reflect on his accomplishments.

Both of us like history, particularly military history. Years ago, Winston had established himself as a modern visionary within international navy circles. Rightfully so! He had thrown overboard old notions of naval traditions, including seniority, which in some obviously overlooked cases he felt equated to senility.

More importantly, he had replaced thirteen-inch battleship guns with fifteen-inchers and changed the fleet from coal to oil. This change not only added lethal firepower but also maneuverability. His ships could now be refueled at sea.

Oddly enough for a navy man, Churchill invented the first tanks deployed in WWI. His distractors called them "Winston's Follies." Drawing on his navy background, he called them land battleships.

Moving from sea and land to air, Churchill also founded the Royal Navy Air Service. Because of his formidable vision, Britain became the first country to equip an airplane with machine guns. And, he coined the word *seaplane* and frequently test piloted the aircraft well into his late thirties. After receiving much pressure from an anguished wife as well as the British Parliament who feared the crash of a prominent military leader, he surrendered his flight suit.

I think back to our first but very brief meeting and wonder if Winston will even remember it. I for one have never forgotten...for rather unpleasant reasons I may add.

We first met in 1918 at a large banquet held in his honor at Gray's Inn, London. Winston was first lord of the Admiralty and clearly relished his "lordly" ceremonial duties, puffing arrogantly on his stubby cigar while circulating like a fan among the lingering smoke and fawning dignitaries.

In appearance Winston's skin had a pinkish glow. His face was smooth, soft, and unwrinkled. His cheeks were full so that he even looked a bit like an overgrown adult baby. His head, rather than his neck, looked attached to his shoulders. But, like a chameleon, he could exchange expression and also "look very stern and forceful." From what I can tell from current photos and newsreels, he looks much the same today, but with less hair and a more portly figure.

At the time we met, I was a young Navy assistant secretary, quite junior in age, rank, and experience to Churchill. I desired to meet him and eagerly wanted a window of opportunity to discuss naval strategy and history with this great man.

Our first introduction proved an embarrassment. He remained unapproachable and seemingly self-centered. Winston treated me like a junior officer, just barely acknowledging my presence! Shame on me, but my ego has never quite forgotten this slight. I hope I don't let old, bitter memories contaminate my discussions with him.

At the time, I had little tolerance and even less appreciation for British pomp and circumstance. I now recognize my views were impeded by my American heritage and culture and sheltered by my pragmatic upstate New York Hudson River Valley upbringing. Now that I am older and a crusty, seasoned politician, I realize how leaders effectively employ ceremony to instill civilian and military pride and confidence in their country. Certainly, Churchill is a master at it, and perversely so is Hitler!

Churchill

To join me on the voyage, I take my most senior military advisors, including Minister of War Production Lord Beaverbrook; Chief of the Imperial General Staff General Sir John Dill, representing the Army;

First Sea Lord Sir Dudley Pound, representing the Navy; and Vice Marshal Sir Wilfred Freeman, representing the Air Force.

We sail on the HMS *Prince of Wales*, the second of our new battleships, along with many of my top military officers and aides. At this stage in the war, I of course need Roosevelt more than he needs me. He knows that and therefore I expect that he will somehow leverage this position during our discussions. But I am not sure exactly how and that worries me.

It is my hope that I can persuade him to discuss high-level strategy and our collective abilities to fight as one, should his nation soon be drawn into direct engagement in the firestorm spreading across all of Europe, Africa, and Russia.

Furthermore, sensing that British resources are stretched to their limits, Japan has begun to encroach on our territories in the Far East. We can ill afford to fight on two fronts, so I also hope that I can persuade Roosevelt to issue strong "cease and desist" warnings to Japan.

To occupy my passage at sea, I take only one book, E. M. Forster's 1924 masterpiece *A Passage to India*, which describes the misunderstandings between Britain and India. In preparation for my meetings with President Roosevelt, I need to contemplate and reflect on the nature of our cultural divides as well as their possible reconciliations. I am fully aware that many Americans still dislike, distrust, or fear British intentions. Nor do they understand or approve of our benevolent form of government, what they label imperialism, in South Africa, India, Indochina, Pakistan, and Hong Kong. This issue could become a sticking point.

During our voyage, Hopkins shares with me what a masterful politician Roosevelt is along with his many accomplishments. I learn that Roosevelt prides himself, justifiably so, in separating tactics from strategy. This is useful information.

And, like myself, he believes that sometimes the end eventually justifies the means. Hopkins tells me that Roosevelt has built a reputation for masterfully juggling through obstacles, issues, and opportunities, "never letting the right hand know what the left hand is doing!" His stealth, wisdom, and charm combine to give his Republican opponents as well as his fellow Democrats hangovers.

According to Hopkins, he also possesses an amazing memory and an inexhaustible reservoir of anecdotes that he serves up with impeccable timing.

Hopkins says he is also very brave. Even though his handicap forces him to move slowly and awkwardly, he does not flinch from meeting the public or fear potential assassins. I learn that while Roosevelt was in Miami in 1933, an assassin fired five shots at him, killing the mayor who sat beside him. The president remained unshaken and went to bed that night sleeping soundly after drinking a glass of whiskey!

Like the assassination attempt, I learn that Roosevelt's response to any occasion is to remain as cool as possible on the exterior, although he may be raging inside. By his demeanor, one can rarely detect what Roosevelt is thinking. By temperament, instead of getting agitated he will "batten down the hatches." If he receives really bad news, he becomes "almost like an iceberg." He has mastered the art of repressing his emotions.

I know that Roosevelt won an unprecedented third presidential election in 1940. But I discover more of the details from Hopkins. He tells me that it is common knowledge that the election had proved the most challenging and divisive of Roosevelt's political career. His decision to seek a third term fired up his opponents, as well as some former supporters, who visualized a "democratic dictatorship." Perhaps I should have known this, but I have been so absorbed in our plight that I have had little time to follow the political events of other countries, other than our enemies.

Throughout the campaign, Hopkins tells me that Roosevelt's opponent, Wendell Willkie, charged that Roosevelt's aid to countries opposing the Axis powers would drag America into the conflict. As far back as 1935, Roosevelt already wore his heart on his sleeve, withdrawing most favored nation status from Germany. Going forward, he responded to every German foreign policy initiative—remilitarizing the Rhineland, annexing Austria, dismembering Czechoslovakia (under pretenses to protect the German minority there)—with punitive duties and restrictions. At the time, Hitler and even many Americans only scorned and criticized these actions.

Hopkins says throughout the 1930s Roosevelt became one of the first great American radio voices . . . articulate, witty, and poignant. Millions of people had never seen a president but now millions hear his "fireside chats," giving them strength and encouragement. His voice remains vibrant and strong. In person, he is evidently a sight to behold. He likes to pose in a chair for photographers, tossing his large head back, a beaming smile on his pear-shaped face, spectacles perched on the end of his nose, eyes twinkling, and cocked in his mouth an ivory cigarette holder with a smoking Camel pointed toward the camera.

I learn, for the most part, that reporters like and respect Roosevelt. Particularly, because he is the first president who doesn't insist on submitting questions in advance of press conferences and he meets with reporters often. He enjoys interacting with them spontaneously and flatters them by saying they are his voice to the American people. Reporters know he is quick on his feet, articulate, and very skillful at diverting negative inquiries. A consummate politician, he can talk forever and not show any of his cards. And if he chooses to show one, it may be only a peek at what's really going on in his mind.

I also extract one more important piece of information from Hopkins. Roosevelt possesses an uncanny ability to "turn empathy on and off at will," as if it poured from a spigot. Hopkins explains that during the Depression there was so much widespread suffering that Roosevelt felt he had to sometimes distance himself from it in order to make professional judgments on matters of a systemic nature affecting the nation. Knowing this helps me better understand the "on and off" signals of encouragement that Roosevelt had been sending me since the beginning of the war.

I can hardly wait to meet this intriguing and engaging man…whatever the outcome. I love characters.

After many days at sea, we finally spot the *Augusta*, idling in the North Atlantic off the coast of Canada. I instruct the battleship HMS *Prince of Wales* to pull beside Roosevelt's ship.

As we approach, a small U.S. Marine band on board the *Augusta* plays "God Save the King." I am deeply touched. Instantly our entire crew cheer and break into wide smiles from the gesture. I shiver in excitement and anticipation of our pending engagement.

I emerge on deck in my favorite blue, ready for battle, with peaked British sailing cap and naval jacket. Personally, I love hats and have collected hundreds for all sorts of special occasions.

Hopkins and I spot Roosevelt immediately. Even with braces on his legs as a result of polio, he stands tall and regal, supported by his son. Both raise their hands to salute me. With a broad smile, I say at last I finally get to meet you, Mr. President, and for the first time of all places here at sea. Then I reach out to shake his hand. Instantly, I notice that his grip is powerful and that his neck and upper body are thick and muscular while his lower body has withered.

Roosevelt is wearing a tan business casual suit. The contrast in our wardrobes as well as ships clearly says that one nation remains at peace. One of my officers also casually observes that the *Prince of Wales*' ready-for-battle camouflaged paint job to obstruct an enemy's view from air, land, and ocean contrasts with the *Augusta*'s peacetime placid shade of gray.

As a token of hospitality, and knowing that Roosevelt likes movies, I present him with a copy of the film *That Hamilton Woman*. I had persuaded one of my best friends, Sir Alexander Korda, a Hungarian Jewish immigrant, to produce the film in April 1941. Laurence Olivier and Vivien Leigh starred in this story about the love affair between Admiral Nelson and Lady Hamilton during the war with Napoleon. I relished personally writing some of Nelson's speeches for the film. I thought that the film would be good for English morale and useful propaganda. The movie depicts Britain's successful resistance to a dictator bent on world domination, just like Hitler.

We spend two days together with Franklin and his dear lads. Our first meeting begins Saturday on board Franklin's heavy cruiser. We lunch around a large table. It is the first time that our most senior British and American commanders and key executive staff meet each other.

I must say the initial introductions prove somewhat awkward. The U.S. commanders and staff are unsure of the exact agenda, and so are mine . . . both second-guessing the purpose of the talks Franklin and I intend to have.

So, Franklin and I must set the stage for discussions. We divide the issues for discussion into two broad categories: the war and the postwar. I know that the latter seems premature, but we need to think optimistically and strategically about our allies and their future interests.

Quite frankly, I think the lunch on board the *Augusta* lacks imagination. Definitely no four- or five-star chefs on board this vessel! Since the time of President Wilson, U.S. Navy vessels have prohibited the consumption of alcohol. Certainly liquid libations would have helped relax and facilitate our initial conversations.

However, we are deeply touched and appreciative when the crew of the *Augusta* presents all of our crew gift boxes containing fresh fruit, cigarettes, cheese, and chocolate. In Britain, all of these items are in extremely short supply. Perhaps a faux pas, but we reciprocate with liquor and their sailors look for an instant like they are ready to mutiny!

Over lunch, I also find Franklin initially stiff and rather reserved. His opaque behavior on such an important occasion mystifies me. I wonder if we have offended the U.S. Navy by offering their crew liquor or committed some other slight? With the stresses from war and life's uncertainty, we think nothing of moderately serving alcohol to our sailors and troops when they are on stand-down.

Tonight, Franklin hosts a formal dinner in the captain's salon and impresses us by personally mixing a batch of potent dry gin martinis. Seems the president is exempt from the U.S. Navy's no-drinking-on-board rule. And quite frankly, based on lunch, the dinner exceeds my expectations. It consists of broiled chicken cooked to perfection, buttered fresh sweet peas (a rarity in Britain these days), a spinach omelet, candied sweet potatoes, tomato salad, assorted cheeses, and chocolate ice cream and cupcakes to die for. We no longer have the luxury of importing chocolate.

Roosevelt

Upon first greeting Winston, I compliment him on a most difficult, courageous, and controversial decision he made to sink on July 3, 1940, a large portion of the French Fleet . . . at its base on the Algerian coast. He had been prime minister only three months when he took that monumental step.

He did this to prevent their fleet from falling into the Nazis' hands. Sadly, almost thirteen hundred French sailors lost their lives. The British also commandeered French ships moored in England. Winston wept upon hearing of the outcome. But, he had no doubt that these ships in the enemy's hands would eventually lead to Britain's ultimate defeat.

Winston had given the French admiral three alternatives: join forces with the British Navy, sail to a neutral port, or scuttle the ships immediately or else he would have to sink their fleet. The admiral did not believe him, nor did Winston trust the admiral's promise to sink his ships if the Nazis tried to claim them.

The "no surrender" agreement that France had in place with England partially influenced Winston's thinking. Neither party could surrender without the approval of the other. England agreed to France's surrender provided they disposed of their navy by selecting one of the three options Winston had presented them. They did nothing and surrendered anyway.

In Winston's mind the stakes were too high to risk a second broken promise. Sinking several French naval ships essentially severed formal diplomatic relations between England and France.

When I heard what Churchill had done, I knew then that he meant to fight to the bitter end no matter the consequence—even if he offended a former ally. His resolve along with Hopkins' most recent reports strengthened my desire to help England and thus finally agreeing to this meeting at sea.

Since we hosted the first two meals together on the *Augusta*, the crew of the *Prince of Wales* insists it is their turn.

By now, our commanders have met individually with their British counterparts to get briefed on the progress of the war and to gain intelligence on the ability of the British to carry the battle forward on their own. We also get their assessments of Germany's strengths, weaknesses, and technological capabilities.

By custom we do not serve alcohol on board Navy vessels . . . at least not openly. However, I relish the offering on the *Prince of Wales*. My emboldened commanders, out of view of their subordinates, follow suit.

We all warm to conversation rather easily. It does not hurt that Winston's vessel serves a masterful selection of his favorite turtle soup, roasted grouse, caviar, bread puddings, and champagne, wine, and brandies. I like his style and clearly Winston courts U.S. favor. To help buoy morale, I do admit that the British approach to feeding its sailors prompts me to reconsider the importance of serving less bland meals on our vessels.

It doesn't take me long to warm to Winston's company. I have to say, though, that he likes to talk, or shall I say orate, a little too much for my preference, going on and on about our countries' shared histories, cultures, and affections for one another.

He lets me know his mother was a U.S. citizen who had been married to a member of the British Parliament. As a result, he claims that he is a child of both great nations.

Winston, or shall I say Lord "Windy," enjoys an enraptured audience. No doubt he is a gregarious man, charming, but somewhat straining to listen to for long stretches.

I do give him credit for his very classy gesture in raising a glass to toast my trusted emissary, closest confidant, and good friend Harry Hopkins for his diligence in matchmaking this event at Placentia Bay.

Prior to our detente onboard our vessels, Harry had travelled to England to engage Churchill in a series of conversations about their ability to resist the Germans and to establish our neutrality while providing them arms. It was really at Harry's encouragement that I meet Churchill off the coast of Newfoundland.

Harry, who sailed with Churchill on the *Prince of Wales*, barely managed to make the voyage after a grueling trip to meet the Russian Communist Party ruler, Joseph Stalin. Along with Churchill and other dignitaries, Harry boarded the *Augusta* clutching his rumpled hat and a battered leather suitcase. It was stuffed with dirty laundry and a large assortment of medicines he constantly took.

Sensing Harry's plight, the captain offered to have the *Augusta*'s crew wash and starch his clothes. The extra starch may have been the only thing that kept Harry upright while at sea!

Harry served as my secretary of commerce and nearly wore himself out in the critical role he played getting the New Deal in place in an attempt to help jumpstart the U.S. economy and put an end to the Depression that raged throughout most of the 1930s. I cannot function without Harry. He provides me an "extra set" of eyes, ears, and legs. Therefore, I now kiddingly call him my "ambassador at large" with no official title since he resigned his cabinet position in fear that his occasionally abrasive manner had been creating enemies who might oppose me in the next election.

After his wife died of cancer in 1937, Harry was a lonely figure. Partially out of sympathy but also for pragmatic reasons, I offered him and his family residence in the White House. To my delight, he accepted.

More than my Vice President Henry Wallace and Secretary of State Cordell Hull, Harry and I truly operate on the same wavelength. He is exceptionally loyal. He unfailingly anticipates my questions and concerns. Just as impressive, he knows when to make deals on his own and when to defer them to me. Another reason I think so dearly of Harry is that he has never craved title or wealth. He never asks for anything. He simply honors the exercise of power and responsibility that I confidently extend him.

Many of my critics nicknamed Harry "FDR's Rasputin." When he comes into my office in the morning, as our private little joke, I sometimes greet him with "And how is Washington's Rasputin doing today?"

Churchill is so amazed by Harry's fine mind, deep insights, and unique ability to frame or define a problem that he has respectfully started referring to him as "Lord Root of the Matter!"

I know my dependency on Harry wears him down, but so often these days he volunteers to take on tasks before I can even bring them up. He's a mind reader. Our nation desperately needs his services and foresight.

Four years ago Harry was diagnosed with cancer and given only a few weeks to live after two-thirds of his stomach had been removed. Realizing how perilous the times were for his country, Harry somehow miraculously recovered . . . perhaps through sheer force of will. He is the force behind the reason we are now meeting. And he saw, perhaps clearer than anyone, how soon the storm raging in Europe and elsewhere might reach our shores. In spite of his doctors' warnings, he somehow thrives on a diet of cigarettes and gallons of coffee. It's a miracle that the man lives and so strongly desires to continue to serve our nation's welfare.

However, Winston has his own equivalent of my Harry, Lord Max Beaverbrook. Beaverbrook was born in Canada. He moved to the United Kingdom and built a journalistic empire. He quickly became a man to reckon with in British politics, and he and Churchill were mostly at odds throughout the 1930s. But Churchill recognized Beaverbrook's entrepreneurial skills and extensive financial connections, and appointed him in charge of wartime production. He is a dealmaker and knows how to manipulate men, resources, and institutions. H. G. Wells once said of Beaverbrook, "If Max ever gets to Heaven, he won't last long. He will be chucked out for trying to pull off a merger between Heaven and Hell after having secured a controlling interest in key subsidiary companies in both places!"

Churchill

After our first meal together, I ask Lord Beaverbrook to see if he can determine why Franklin seemed so formal and reserved during our introductions. He quietly approaches Hopkins on the side with my question. Hopkins, always a forthright person and a critical facilitator on the world stage, informs my aide that Franklin and I had met some twenty-three years ago in London. He shares with him that he knew that Roosevelt felt I had appeared condescending at a banquet, treating him like a junior officer. Hopkins counsels that I should try hard to erase this image. I cannot honestly recall our first meeting—perhaps blurred now by time and a river of fine brandy and Scotch whiskey. But, I know I have to change his impression before we break anchor.

Britain—no, I mean the world—has a higher call to duty for Roosevelt, and I must resolve any past grievances as best I can. He has already risked much of his reputation to provide us life-sustaining support while defying his adversaries at home. I cannot lose this precious moment in time to forge stronger bonds between our two countries.

As a side note, the private meeting between Lord Beaverbrook and Hopkins proves very fortuitous. They begin to form a very close working relationship and admiration for one another's skills that I think may yield future benefits. In many respects these two men are very much alike in how they tackle problems and think through solutions . . . so much so that I wonder if they have a genetic link.

Just as I feared, Franklin and I spar over the topics of British colonialism and the most favored nation trade agreement that exists among members of the British Empire. Neither of us holds back our views, and our relationship grows tense.

As a possibly veiled condition of providing Britain further help, Franklin presses me to begin to set the stage for ending colonialism and promoting free trade. He insinuates that the empire's existing trade agreements are keeping the colonial people of India, Africa, and Asia backward and poor.

Tempers begin to flair and I rebut that he should reflect upon the history of the U.S.'s double standard, considering the U.S. expansionist efforts governing the Philippines, Hawii, Puerto Rico, Alaska, the institution of the Monroe Doctrine, and invasion of Cuba.

The result becomes a temporary stalemate, with some mutual

concessions, which eventually leads after much back-and-forth wordsmithing into what we decide to call the Atlantic Charter . . . a most significant document.

Our military staffs also disagree about how the war should be conducted in Europe. We British, shaped by memories of millions of men led to slaughter in World War I trenches, wish to avoid a direct invasion of the European mainland. We feel strongly that the Germans can be defeated by superior air power, mastery of the oceans, and indirect engagements in which we whittle and wear them down as they overextend themselves.

In contrast, the U.S., particularly General George Marshall, believes the lesson of World War I remains obvious—that massive land invasion through German-occupied Europe and into Berlin is again the only way to defeat a stubborn, hardened enemy.

Since the U.S. is not directly in the fight shedding blood, we do not welcome nor embrace Marshall's view.

We also ask for more munitions, airplanes, and ships than the U.S. can currently physically produce. Our requests put General Marshall in a bind. Congress has assigned him, as chief of staff of the U.S. forces, the onerous task of deciding which military equipment to send abroad to aid the Allies and which to keep at home to build up American defenses. No matter what I ask for or Roosevelt wants to do to help, Marshall has to sign off on military aid. His position forces him to straddle the fence between the interventionists who want to ship as much military hardware as possible to the Allies and the isolationists who put America first. He is caught in a vice . . . between his commander-in-chief, Roosevelt, and Congress.

I think a joint Sunday morning worship service on board the *Prince of Wales* might help cement our relationship and make amends for the slight Roosevelt remembers from so long ago. I spend a lot of time planning the details with our ship's chaplain. The result becomes a deeply moving expression of our common faith and values, as expressed through scripture and hymns. The crews of both nations intermingle during the service, discovering to their mutual surprise that they and their families have grown up with the same familiar verses and hymns.

Setting aside some areas of disagreement, I do succeed in my endeavor to win Franklin's good graces. He apologizes that the timing is still not right for the U.S. to enter the war in Europe. He pledges that he is an ardent friend of Great Britain, as well as my friend, and will do whatever he can to provide Britain arms, ships, and planes.

As a result of our time together in Newfoundland, I find encouraging Franklin's assurances that we may soon be in the same boat if he has his way. But, he also says that the path in that direction still remains a very politically complicated and divisive issue at home.

At this time, Franklin still tells the American people that he will do everything he can to avoid a war—one that he knows that they are not yet prepared to fight. He is a complex and formidable man, in a delicate situation, working both sides of the aisle while walking down the middle.

Until he can persuade the American public of the values they will be fighting to preserve if they join Britain in battle, I am thrilled that Franklin has volunteered to offer Britain even more food and weapons. He also pledges to replace the British forces in Iceland with American troops. In addition, he says that his armed forces will assume responsibility for air and sea patrols around the Iceland waters. That's major for us because it will free up to fifty British warships for patrols elsewhere.

On parting, he requests that I continue to send him as much intelligence as I can on the war and to keep him posted on the fighting spirit and resolve of the British people. I think to myself as we say our good-byes that Franklin is perhaps the most memorable and complex man I have ever encountered . . . and in my lifetime I have met quite a few exceptional men and women. When engaging him in conversation, he is high-spirited, exhibiting a lively effervescence and aura of optimism that bubbles out of him like a freshly opened bottle of fine champagne.

Our joint meetings over a two-day period proved intense and somewhat frustrating. My military staff wanted to discuss in much more detail the strategies and tactics related to the current war. On a contingency basis should the U.S. enter the war, they also wanted to explore options regarding how we might possibly combine our military forces into a joint effort. Clearly their U.S. counterparts were not yet prepared for such elaborate discussions.

Before we leave for England, General Marshall, readily acknowledges that the U.S. is scrambling to establish a wartime footing and the process is chaotic They are still passing through the early stages of assembling and equipping an army, organizing a command structure, implementing a new draft system, and orchestrating efforts between their army, air force, and navy. This explains their military command's reluctance to either give much advice or enter into collaborative discussions.

We set sail for home. I assure my commanders and cabinet that the meeting has gone as well as can be expected. The American pudding needs to bake just a little bit longer before being ready to serve.

During our return to England, the *Prince of Wales* plows through some extremely rough seas. In a mood to relax, my staff and I play backgammon. We also watch a Laurel and Hardy movie called *Saps at Sea*, which we hope isn't an omen of our meeting with Roosevelt, and chuckle at Donald Duck cartoons. As some of you women may observe, even grown men never quite grow up. I arrive home content, rested, and cautiously optimistic for a stronger British and U.S. alliance.

Roosevelt

While in Newfoundland I gain quite a different, more favorable, impression of Winston. Occasionally he taxes my capacity to listen to him pontificate. But, it dawns on me that by nature he is much more expressive and eloquent than I am. As if to make up for some past slight, I sense that he has become solicitous, working hard to earn my respect and make a good impression. Perhaps he becomes increasingly verbose when he is nervous. Even though he conceals it, I recognize how much stress he is under and how important this meeting is to his country.

Hopkins briefs Winston and me on the outcome of his trip to Russia. He informs us that he has extracted a commitment from Joseph Stalin that the Russians will gladly throw their forces behind any country who fights Hitler. Even though almost half of Russia's total population and production capabilities have succumbed to the invasion, Stalin demonstrates an iron will. He assures Hopkins that with material help from the U.S. and Britain that the Russian people and the Red Army will repel the Nazis' attack.

Churchill says that he has always been opposed to communism. Plus, he doesn't personally like or trust old Uncle Joe, as I call Stalin. Fortunately, Churchill agrees to compromise his instincts and principles to gain another ally.

We are both curious what the man is like. Hopkins says Stalin possesses a talent for detail as well as an ability to frame and state issues clearly and concisely. He has a sense of humor and laughs readily, but he can quickly turn stern and dour.

He dresses simply, wearing a plain gray tunic, no medals on his chest, and baggy trousers stuffed into shiny black leather boots that rise to his knees. His office is huge but unpretentious and uncluttered, with a Spartan-looking desk covered with multiple telephones and push buttons to summon personnel . . . all indicating just how centralized his authority and command structure is.

With the build of a classic football tackle or guard, Stalin is rather short but very thick boned and broad shouldered . . . a dominant physical presence. Hidden below bushy eyebrows and a black mustache, Stalin's teeth are stained yellow from a lifetime of smoking, poor diet, and liberal consumption of vodka. His face is pale and scarred from smallpox.

Until now, we were very worried that Stalin might cut a deal, falling for another deceptive peace overture from Hitler. He had already been duped once by Hitler's promises that Germany would not invade beyond Poland's borders into Russia.

Hopkins assures us that having met him, Stalin, even though reputedly quite ruthless, is too pragmatic not to keep his word. Plus Stalin, possibly responsible himself for the death of millions of people who opposed him, now believes Hitler fails even a minimum moral standard as a human being. He feels that the Nazis are an "antisocial force" in the world that must be eliminated at all cost. Churchill and I chuckle at the irony of Stalin's brash statements yet concur with his observations.

During his trip, Hopkins learned firsthand from Russian generals and party members that they defer to Stalin on all matters. His authority is unquestioned. He is the only one to deal with and the only one who will make commitments. Hopkins describes Stalin as a "forthright, rough, tough Russian partisan through and through, thinking always first of Russia." Fortunately, Hopkins says that he can be approached in a direct and frank manner.

Regretfully, at our meeting in Newfoundland, I cannot yet give Churchill all the assurances that he hoped for and that I would like to have provided. The U.S. simply isn't ready or equipped to come to the immediate and direct defense of Great Britain. To Churchill's chagrin, I have sidestepped any kind of declaration of a formal alliance that could give my isolationist opponents back home the cannon fodder to accuse me of entering into an unconstitutional agreement with Great Britain and its colonial empire.

I do tell Churchill that the U.S. shares his deep concern about Japan and will employ all available diplomatic measures to keep them in check. We both agree that Japan is another ticking time bomb that needs to be defused before it explodes.

Back home, I dare not fully play my hand without first doing more arm pulling and leg twisting of key influencers in Congress and American industry. We are ever so close. But, I am still stuck in the mode of two dance steps forward, one back, until I can steer American sentiment to the reality that, as a matter of principle, our nation cannot long remain on the sidelines regarding affairs in Europe.

So, my fishing excursion up the coast of Maine nets bigger fish than I could have hoped. I set sail back to Washington with the invaluable knowledge that the Brits and the Russians will cooperate on a joint response to Hitler's growing appetite for European dominance and suppression.

If the U.S. joins the war, I feel strongly that the three of us, acting in unison, can tip the balance of scale in our favor. This will be one of the aces I hope to play with Congress and the American people when the opportune time arrives.

As we depart, I'll never forget a poem recited by Churchill that had been etched on the wall by a Jewish prisoner in a Cologne concentration camp. He heard about it from the Jewish underground movement.

The poem, he said, reflects his own view in the face of the horrible events unfolding around him. With great emotion, he quotes two of the passages:

I believe in the sun even when it's not shining.
I believe in love when I don't feel it.
I believe in God, even if God is silent."
May there someday be sunshine.
May there someday be happiness.
May there someday be love.
May there someday be peace....

I must admit that the fact that I pull this fishing trip off without the press first discovering it gives me a sense of boyish satisfaction. I can still picture them watching my double cruise out to sea on a fake fishing expedition. Fooled them this time! Can't wait to hear them whine.

I am particularly proud of the Atlantic Charter. This document's general language that Winston and I thrashed out at sea, after much disagreement, will soon be announced to the world. We pledge our mutual support to create a world in which freedom and democracy will replace repression and tyranny. The charter essentially grants that all peoples may ultimately choose the form of government under which they may live.

Since he is so desperate for any kind of additional support from the U.S. in this time of crisis, I am not sure that Winston fully grasps or wants to grasp that the Atlantic Charter potentially sets the stage for unraveling his extensive and beloved British Empire. The agreement holds particularly strong implications for India and other colonies in Asia. Of course it would have been diplomatically unwise of me to spell out what this new world vision possibly means. Rightfully so, Winston is so focused on his country's survival that he struggles with implications of what a victory might mean after the war . . . so he is not particularly interested in the fine print. Perhaps I still have that luxury since we are not at war.

Perhaps of greater importance, Winston and I have formed a bond at sea. We broke the ice. We each have a better grasp of what motivates the other. Our military staffs have begun to probe and share their concerns and needs in case we become allies in arms. I depart certain that Churchill is a man I can work with and trust.

Did I mention that my little Scottish terrier Fala joined us on the cruise? I knew that Churchill liked dogs so I thought Fala, of British heritage herself, might contribute to foreign relations. On the trip home Fala starts to look like a plucked chicken! When out of eyesight, our own sailors begin snipping off her locks for souvenirs. This infuriates me. If I could have caught the culprits in the act, I'd have thrown them in the brig for violating government property.

Winston Churchill, Franklin Roosevelt, and his sons Franklin
Jr. (left) and Elliott aboard USS *Augusta* at Placentia Bay,
Newfoundland, August 1941. *U.S. Naval Heritage Command*

Winston Churchill and Franklin Roosevelt at a church service
aboard HMS *Prince of Wales*, Placentia Bay, Newfoundland,
August 1941. *U.S. Naval History Heritage Command*

USS *Augusta*, on which Roosevelt sailed to meet Churchill in Newfoundland. *Department of the Navy Historical Center*

HMS *Prince of Wales*, on which Churchill sailed to meet Roosevelt in Newfoundland. *U.S. Naval History Heritage Command*

Chapter Two

"GUESS WHO'S COMING TO THE WHITE HOUSE, DEAR"

December 7, 1941

Churchill

This evening in London, I dined in my home with U.S. Envoy Averell Harriman and Ambassador John Winant. The BBC radio program playing quietly in the background fed us our steady wartime diet of news intermingled with music. Listening to the soothing music of Artie Shaw's "Star Dust," Tommy Dorsey's "I'll Never Smile Again," and Coleman Hawkins' "Body and Soul," we were as relaxed as three people can possibly be with the constant threat of nighttime air raids lurking overhead. The curtains were pulled and the flickering candles on the dinner table created a warm, soft glow reflecting off our wine glasses and the polished silverware.

As usual, while falling short of begging, between bites I continued to press them for more aid from the United States . . . more food, more clothing, more munitions and arms, more medicines, more fuel . . . all the things that have been depleted since we began fighting Germany and Italy while also trying to aid the Russians.

Our quiet conversations were suddenly shattered by disturbing and stunning news coming from the BBC's newscaster that Japan had just attacked Pearl Harbor.

On a Sunday morning that dawned bright and sunny, Japan, without any forewarning, caught by total surprise dozens of American warships resting at port. As details begin to filter in, we are all dismayed to learn that six battleships have just been sunk, three light cruisers and four destroyers incapacitated, and three hundred aircraft badly damaged or destroyed. Early estimates project that over three thousand Americans may be killed and thousands more injured.

With a jumble of thoughts spiraling through my head, I realize I must immediately call President Roosevelt to express my country's condolences and convey solidarity. I can personally relate to the pain and horror that will now confront his people too. I know I must communicate optimism in spite of the coming ordeals.

With Harriman and Winant grimly sitting anxiously by my side, I give Roosevelt a call at 9 p.m. London time and he shortly comes on the line. He confirms what we just heard on the BBC news. Before I can convey my deep concerns and consternation, he bursts the conversation, saying, "Winston, they have attacked us at Pearl Harbor and we are now all in the same boat. A boat that cannot and will not be sunk!" Carefully choosing my words, I respond that we will join him at the altar by declaring war on Japan.

I think to myself we will now become a union that cannot and must not be broken, with all the inherent compromises that exist in any enduring marriage.

While on the telephone, Roosevelt shares with me that intelligence reports he received today estimate that had Japanese pilots flown further inland, they would have destroyed a vast supply of munitions and possibly crippled America's whole Pacific fleet. He calmly continues to tell me that this worst-case scenario might have led to a mass evacuation from Hawaii. Japan's single-mindedness and lack of better intelligence seems to have missed completing a knockout punch. Thank Providence.

Roosevelt says that his cabinet is right now heading to the White House. Grabbing at historical precedence, he recognizes that the impending meeting will be the most important one with the cabinet since Abraham Lincoln met with his at the outbreak of the Civil War. After he confers with his cabinet and Congress, Roosevelt plans to inform the American people that they are now at war with Japan. He expects that

Germany will join their Japanese ally and also declare war on the U.S., thus resolving his country's reluctance to join the fray in Europe.

Roosevelt

My first reaction to the attack on Pearl Harbor is one of disbelief, followed by a momentary sense of shame and embarrassment that it has happened under my administration.

We were aware that Japan's defiance toward us was stiffening and that fighting could break out. It is now evident that we have misplayed our hand by initially appealing only to their sense of humanity while all along Japan further encroached on China and Korea.

As they continued their expansion, we responded with embargos on oil, copper, and scrap metal and tougher military threats if they did not back off. Prior to their invasion of China, we provided Japan close to 80 percent of their oil, 74 percent of their scrap metal, and over 90 percent of their copper requirements. Then we closed their access to the Panama Canal. Their dependency on us may have accelerated the attack on Pearl Harbor in order to buy time to seek alternative sources of oil and other minerals. With hindsight, now I wonder if we should have anticipated such a reaction and better prepared for it. Our isolationists certainly would have bellyached.

Throughout the year we received reports that the Japanese were trying to assess our military strength in the Pacific. Now we are caught with our pants down; we never expected that, undetected, Japan could extend so quickly its military might as far as Hawaii. Right up to the time of the attack, their ambassadors were still pretending to negotiate with us. All the while, resorting to violence had become their preferred course of action.

As we become increasingly aware of the extent of the devastation, quite honestly I consider firing all my handpicked chiefs of staffs. It seems to me that everything these men have done or not done to ready us for conflict in the Pacific has failed wretchedly with the bashing of the whole fleet anchored in Pearl Harbor along with the crippling of our air force, which never left the ground. But, I honestly ask myself: Who could I replace them with? What would it do to the nation's confidence, and what is the extent of my accountability? I had set the tone of our negotiations with the Japanese, as well as the embargoes, by trying to maintain a higher moral ground when on their side none existed.

Late in the afternoon, I collect myself and call my personal secretary, Grace Tully, to dictate to her the message I plan to deliver to Congress tomorrow. I will ask them to respond by declaring war on Japan. I decide to keep my perfunctory message deliberately short, although members of my cabinet argue for more background information and detail. I overrule them and leave it at only 390 words. I believe the invasion itself provides all the evidence necessary for Congress to act upon.

And candidly and politically speaking, a short address, to the point, may keep any member of the House or the Senate from finding an excuse to criticize me or my administration for "not having done more to appease or dissuade the Japanese government from going to war." I am hoping they will see that we have no other recourse other than, without delay, to gather our wits and rise up and beat Japan.

In the evening I meet with key members of Congress in the Oval Office to share with them the scope of the attack and to get their official blessing to meet with Congress. While there, more bad news trickles in. We learn that Malaya, Hong Kong, Bangkok, and Singapore have also been bombed. The fact that we are not alone in being surprised and hideously attacked gives us no solace.

Shortly after midnight, I am exhausted and still angry and distraught, but I feel it is my duty to meet with my good friend, CBS reporter Edward R. Murrow. I ask him if he believes our nation will rally like the British did when they were attacked. He assures me that they will, and it will prove a powerfully countervailing force that Japan will eventually regret. I trust his judgment and feel for the pulse and spirit of the American people. With some relief, at 1 a.m. I call it a day . . . the longest day of my life!

December 11, 1941

Churchill

Today Germany announced that they supported their Japanese friends by declaring war on the United States. Clearly, these two countries are collaborators, and I doubt that the invasion of Pearl Harbor surprised Hitler. Within hours, America responded with its own declaration, and a state of war now exists between these two mighty nations.

Two concerns weigh heavily upon me. First, I fear that Germany will intensify the pace to defeat us before the U.S. can marshal any significant effort to join us on the continent.

Second, I have a sense from diplomatic communications between our two countries that the U.S. will allocate most of its initial efforts to strike back at Japan. I can't blame them for wanting revenge as soon as possible. But, this would delay the U.S. from plunging into the inferno that we Brits, the last lion still standing in Europe, have been battling essentially by ourselves the last two years.

Therefore, it has become urgent that I meet personally once again with Roosevelt. I know that if such a meeting is to occur, I will have to travel to him, as the U.S. cannot spare to have their new wartime leader present anywhere else but in its nation's capital. But in preparation for this trip I am going to have to go back to school on this man to convince him of the imperative of closely orchestrated cooperation. I tell myself that I must learn even more about him than cupid ever did the fancies, quirks, and desires of his beloved. And I know just the people who can help. Two of them just had dinner with me and the other, Harry Hopkins, has already been immeasurably helpful to both Roosevelt and myself.

While I abhor the severe American losses at Pearl Harbor, I must confess a deep relief that our friends across the Atlantic will now join us in the fight against these two most formidable tyrants. I realize we cannot win the war in Europe without U.S. participation—even if their active-duty army at the time is smaller than Romania's. Forgive me for saying this, but I go to bed tonight to sleep "the sleep of the saved and thankful."

Roosevelt

Today I get a second call from Churchill saying that he needs to meet with me personally to help convince the American people that the number one objective of the war should be the defeat of Germany, followed by Japan. He wants to come to America to have these discussions, and presses his case for a visit with great urgency. He worries that the U.S.

will devote all its energies to defeating Japan, and until then leave the Brits and the Russians to fend for themselves against Germany and Italy.

I speak frankly with Churchill and try to discourage his visit. With the war only a few days old, I feel his plan is premature. Our Congress, military, and citizens need precious time to assimilate these shockingly recent events and to prepare themselves for war.

With all of this on my mind, I tell Churchill that under these circumstances I do not think that we can afford the immediate distractions of a visiting head of state—even one such as him, now our principal ally. Plus, I know that many of my top command and staff, including General George Marshall and Admiral Stark, feel we need to first settle our own basic war strategy and production and shipping priorities before any meeting with Churchill. They fear that Great Britain will try to meddle in those decisions, influenced as they are by their own priorities.

Churchill will not to be put off, and I get a sense that he has already packed his bags. He stresses the importance and urgency of our key commanders meeting face to face to begin coordinating military efforts and resources. To up the ante, he says he will bring most of the key people he had with him during our August rendezvous off the Canadian coast, including Minister of Supply Lord Beaverbrook, First Sea Lord Sir Alfred Pound, Chief of Air Staff Charles Porter, Field Marshall Sir John Dill, and Sir Charles Wilson, his personal physician and friend.

He presses his position despite the fact that his beloved HMS *Prince of Wales*, the battleship on which he sailed to our meeting in Newfoundland, was sunk on December 9 along with the HMS *Repulse* off the coast of Malaya by a Japanese aircraft carrier. Eight hundred and forty British sailors lost their lives. These sinkings meant that Japan now dominated every ocean, except the Atlantic.

Knowing in due course how badly Churchill wants to retaliate in the Pacific, I do not relent to his demands to visit unless I can get him to agree to several provisos. We must begin the dance of give and take right now!

First, I know full well that Churchill is already sixty-seven years old. Since the beginning of the war, he has been maintaining an exhausting pace that would have severely taxed a much younger man. He is our senior statesman of the war . . . four years older than Stalin, eight years older than me, nine years older than Mussolini, and fifteen years older than

Hitler. To add to his physical limitations, the journey across the Atlantic in winter will not be pleasant, nor without risk of being torpedoed. In light of all of that, I insist that he and some of his top military staff and advisors stay in the White House to celebrate Christmas with us, his American cousins, and that he not plan to leave any sooner than after New Year's Day. We will have much to discuss and I want to make sure that the man remains well rested. Plus, with my handicap, it will be much easier and convenient for us to access one another on the spur of the moment under the same roof.

Second, I tell him I will arrange for him to address Congress but that he needs to be very well prepared to explain his rationale for prioritizing the defeat of Germany over Japan.

Lastly, I add, while together we should jointly speak to our respective citizens to strengthen their resolve that allied together, on both sides of the Atlantic, we can and will defeat our enemies.

After much discussion of these and other matters, and in spite of my initial objections, by force of his personality Churchill prevails. He ends the call by telling me that he will set sail on December 12 on board the HMS *Duke of York*. That's tomorrow! Clearly Britain has learned from its wartime experience how to expedite decision making and convert it to action. My country has much to learn about chain of command when life and death is at stake, and I take notice.

Churchill

We have been seven days aboard the HMS *Duke of York* on a journey that should have lasted five. The captain estimates that it will be at least two more days before we arrive in Washington. Thank goodness for this stout ship, a sister to the HMS *George V* and HMS *Prince of Wales*. Each of these was one of our three most modern and best-equipped battleships, but the *Prince of Wales* now sadly rests on the floor of the Pacific.

Many sailors believe the North Atlantic in the wintertime becomes the roughest ocean in the world. We are not allowed to go on deck because of the incessant pounding the ship takes while sailing at her maximum speed of twenty-five knots to avoid detection.

Mountainous, snarly looking black waves come straight up over the bow and then crash down on the deck so severely that several crewmembers have broken their arms and legs. Strong gales gust up fifty to sixty miles an hour, creating an unnerving howling sound that penetrates the upper deck. At times it feels like we are in a submarine, not one of the world's largest battleships.

Midway through our voyage, I telegraph my wife Clementine that the weather we are experiencing at sea imprisons us in the bowels of the ship and if you go on deck you'll drown.

To insulate myself from a very unpleasant voyage, I spend most of the days in bed contemplating the strategy I will employ to steer Roosevelt and Congress toward my points of view. I also occupy my time writing position papers and responding to cables from the war front. I also find time to partake of my precious supply of favorite Cuban cigars, and to down copious amounts of brandy and Scotch whiskey for inspiration. It also helps to mellow out the trip.

During the voyage, I have important discussions with Lord Beaverbrook. Given his experience and success in overseeing wartime production, I tell him that I would like him to determine with the Americans how much we can jointly produce, who should produce it, how production will be allocated, and lastly who controls the process—the civilian authorities or the military? I encourage him to chip away at them as hard as he can without breaking his pick.

I consider Beaverbrook's task the next toughest, aside from the one I am assuming of getting America to do: prioritize its latent military might on Europe first, then Japan. Beaverbrook is the logical choice. He brilliantly ramped up air production from a dozen or so fighters a month shortly before the Battle of Britain began to hundreds. Aside from our exhausted RAF fighter pilots, he is as responsible as anyone for victory in the conflict that raged from July to October 1940 . . . the first military campaign in history to be fought entirely in the air, mostly over the British Isles.

I also received the bad news that the Japanese landed in northern Borneo on December 17 and the next day occupied Hong Kong Island. We dare not lose Singapore.

I continue to dictate a stream of memoranda on my views going forward, particularly about Russia. Even though events in the Pacific spread us thin, I believe very strongly that supplies to Russia from both Britain and the U.S. must be sustained at all costs. We must hold our influence over Stalin in order to incorporate their massive raw military power into our combined effort to win the war in Europe. I fear that if Russia gets knocked out of the war, the Germans will descend on Britain in full force before America can become fully mobilized. We must not let this happen.

There is one bright spot in this interminable journey. In the evenings, no matter how badly the ship rolls, I do get to watch films with the captain and my ministers. My favorite diversion thus far has been *Blood and Sand*, a bullfighting drama released just this year starring Rita Hayworth, Tyrone Powers, and Anthony Quinn.

Blood and Sand is such a beautiful and artistically filmed movie. Our British film industry stopped making films at the outbreak of the war, so we find it refreshing and thrilling to see a movie this new. And, what can I say about Rita Hayworth, the seductress? Perhaps it was already too much time at sea, but we sailors find her drop-dead gorgeous.

The plot also held my attention . . . almost as much as Rita. It's the story of a rags-to-riches bullfighter played by the talented Tyrone Powers who only wants to become a gifted bullfighter like his father, who died in the ring. And so he does.

With fame in his hand, the son loses perspective and succumbs to the charms of another woman, who dumps him for a fresh and upcoming bullfighter played by Anthony Quinn. With the help of his forgiving wife, the son pulls himself out of the gutter. To prove himself once again, he braves one more round in the ring before retiring, and like his father is gored by the bull and dies.

Over a nightcap in the privacy of my room, I later reflect on the parallels of *Blood and Sand* in my life. I think to myself this movie reminds me of my father, who came so close to becoming prime minister and failed . . . due to his philandering and other shortcomings. The other thought I have as prime minister is that like the bullfighter one dare not soar like an eagle and then crash timidly like a tiny canary.

With great opportunity comes great risk. I am willing to risk great personal failure and agony to save my country. But, I am not willing to risk my marriage because my partner is not only gorgeous herself but also keeps me anchored.

We also watched *The Fighting 69th* with James Cagney, *Santa Fe Trail* with Ronald Reagan and Errol Flynn, *North West Mounted Police* with Gary Cooper, and *Boom Town* with Clark Gable and Spencer Tracy.

Now that America is at war, I make a note to myself to discuss with Roosevelt redeploying all this enormously rich acting talent to help make morale-boosting films, promote bond sales, and produce training and educational films. I have no doubt that most would gladly do this with little expectations in pay.

Our onboard film reels have given us a healthy dose of American culture and slang. And, I think they might help us quickly find some common ground with our American counterparts when we meet them in Washington. If nothing else, we can jumpstart our interactions by facilitating a little social conversation about film clips and actors.

To the amazement of my colleagues, I am one of the few passengers unaffected by seasickness, and I am always up to watching the action unfold on a screen without getting nauseous.

December 19, 1941

Roosevelt

Today I received a wire from Churchill aboard the *Duke of York* relaying his thoughts on an agenda for the upcoming talks. His wish list of topics to discuss and resolve includes framing a joint strategy, launching immediate military actions, and deploying joint forces, and then longer-term goals for building and equipping a modern fighting force.

During our August meeting in Newfoundland with Churchill, his ministers, and military staff, I had felt we were unprepared and ill equipped for the in-depth conversations they wanted to have with us and somewhat bulldozed by their mission and agenda. This time, I am not about to let the British dominate our upcoming Washington talks!

To that end, I immediately convene a meeting with Admirals King, Stark, and Nimitz, General Marshall, Secretary of War Stimson, Secretary of the Navy Knox, and my presidential advisor Hopkins. I order them to work around the clock to prepare an American equivalent of Churchill's submission.

Never before have two great nations contemplated so thoroughly combining and integrating resources in a global conflict of such scale. No historical template exists for such an undertaking. As we set forth to forge a united Anglo-American war effort, my American colleagues anticipate significant friction between ourselves and the British over such things as cultural differences and division of resources, responsibilities, and leadership. Regarding the latter, of course, our military command would like to prevail on these matters.

While somewhat sympathetic, I know I cannot let these comments go unchecked.

After a prolonged period of silence while I scratch Fala's ears while she sits on my lap, I look up at my war cabinet and firmly communicate that we must let differences in style not get in the way of substance. I stress that where we have strengths we should remain willing to lead, but where we have weaknesses we should be willing to follow.

I go as far as to say I know that some of your fathers and their ancestors may have harbored grudges toward the British for this or that reason, even dating back to colonial times or their arrogant presence as the world's foremost navy power throughout most of the last century. I bang the table and say it stops in this room today. The British are now our allies, we share a common language and democratic values, and most importantly they have been survivors in this deadly war. We have much to learn from their successes and failures engaging our mutual enemies. Perhaps I go too far when I tell them to remove their egos from their uniforms. I apologize but ask each one individually if they understand my message or have any grievances to air. None do. Meeting over.

I still have not told Eleanor that Churchill will be arriving. Up to this point, I have only casually told her that we may be having some guests drop in on us, and I instructed her to convert the Monroe Room on the second floor into an office so that maps could be hung on the walls and spread out on tables. I added that she must prepare for our guests, unknown in number, to stay over Christmas and to include them in all our plans. I suggested that she also have an adequate number of Christmas presents. I emphasized that she should stock an ample supply of very good champagne and brandy in the house and plenty of Scotch whiskey. Then I said, by the way, we might need to set the table tonight for twenty or so guests.

For security reasons, I also have not yet informed her that Churchill and five or so of his aides and key military advisors will be sleeping in our house. It isn't that I don't trust her. But, any commotion on a grand scale might cause the Nazis and Japs to speculate on its purpose or, worse yet, threaten the prime minister's voyage, with all his top echelon of military advisors on board. Silently, I think to myself there will be hell to pay when I reveal the names of her household guests.

December 21, 1941

Roosevelt

Even an old salty sea dog craves dry land after a long journey. The original plan called for the HMS *Duke of York* to sail up the Potomac so that Churchill could disembark a short drive from the White House. However, my friend had grown impatient after having spent ten days on a turbulent sea that should have taken half as much time. He insisted on putting to shore at Hampton Roads and flying the remaining 120 miles or so to Washington.

Now that Churchill's arrival has been advanced almost a day, and given that I was about to greet him at the airport, I am forced to confess to Eleanor today. Ta-da, surprise, the prime minister of Great Britain himself will be our guest, along with his entourage!

Perhaps because of the combination of my disabilities, responsibilities, and clandestine nature, Eleanor has, out of necessity, become a flexible and accommodating wife. But she goes bonkers when I inform her that the prime minister will be sharing the house with us for perhaps two to three weeks. Her scolding, angry voice bounces off the White House walls and echoes down the hallways. Sheepishly, I peek at the nearby staff who are all grimacing. She remains agitated most of the day. I hope that if I pour her a good stiff cocktail in the evening it might help sedate her.

In fairness to Eleanor, let me be clear. She doesn't resent Churchill coming. She is just plain furious with me for not alerting her in sufficient time to fully prepare for his arrival. Women are kind of touchy about little things like that. She had given several of the White House staff time off for the holidays. Now she has to find them and call them back ... perhaps ruining their own holiday plans. We will need all hands on deck to prepare for the imminent encampment of the British prime minister and his key advisors. Perhaps rationalizing the whole thing, I shrug it off as a higher calling to duty.

I confess, I enjoy a little spontaneity once in a while just to keep everyone on their toes. After thirty-six years of marriage, I am not good at coming up with surprise Christmas presents for Eleanor. This one, however, is a doozy!

Churchill

When we land today at the new National Airport, Roosevelt and Hopkins are parked on the tarmac waiting to greet me. I have not expected them to be there. Considering that Roosevelt's legs are paralyzed, I am deeply touched by the effort he makes to personally receive me. It is truly an honor that catches me off guard.

Instinctively, I reach out to clasp Roosevelt's hand. His grip is strong, reassuring, and as steady as his eye contact. This brilliant gesture, at which he seems so skillful, telegraphs a message how much he welcomes me to his nation's capital.

Upon departing the airport, Roosevelt playfully explains we are riding in one of two government-owned 1938 Cadillacs that he named, because of their bulk, after great ocean liners—*Queen Elizabeth* and *Queen Mary*. In choosing the *Elizabeth* for the ride to the White House, he smiles and says he thought it was appropriate for one of the queens to provide the British prime minister transportation back to the White House.

Both of the cars weigh almost eight thousand pounds and are equipped with a full arsenal of ammunition, two-way radios, and heavy-duty generators. He tells me that we may not ride in these cars too many more times since neither has armor protection or bulletproof glass. Now that the nation is at war, the Secret Service worries that there might be attempts to assassinate the nation's leaders. However, our enemies won't learn about my visit for several hours. So, no one seems terribly concerned about the short trip back to the White House.

While riding back to the White House, Roosevelt tells me it was a thrill for him to see a head of state emerge from an airplane, and quite adventuresome at that! He says he needs to rethink future travel arrangements since no American president has ever flown on an airplane while in office. I can see the wheels spinning in his head—he is warming fast to the idea of becoming the first American president to fully embrace this modern-day mode of transportation.

In route, I ask Franklin to demonstrate the quality of the car's radio speakers. Coincidentally, on comes "Boogie Woogie Bugle Boy" sung by the Andrews Sisters. The tune, released in January 1941, is quite catchy and most appropriate since they were singing about the draft, which had been implemented in September of 1940. Franklin taps his hand to the beat, seemingly enjoying the patriotic spirit of the piece.

Roosevelt

While waiting to greet Churchill at the airport, I ponder over my initial hesitancy for him to come so soon to the United States. Because the immediate tasks ahead following Pearl Harbor seemed so enormous, I don't think I was ready to get my mind around the value of his visit. As the fog of war begins to clear, I start to realize the faster we get together to jointly plot a grand strategy to challenge our enemies, the more reassuring it will be for citizens on both sides of the Atlantic. This meeting now seems inevitable, a hand of fate.

As his plane touches down on the tarmac, I think to myself that old man Churchill once again proved himself a visionary, as he has done so many times before. He correctly predicted the events in Europe and even Japan. To him, the script we were now cast in as allies was written when Hitler first published in 1925 the text of his *Mein Kampf*. Churchill clearly foresaw where the founding text of Nazism would eventually lead.

Therefore, I give Winston the warmest possible welcome to make him feel that his long journey is already worthwhile. I also want to convey to him my full support of the "Anglo-American marriage ceremony" that is about to unfold over the next several weeks in the White House and Washington, D.C.

Churchill

My Redcoat British ancestors tried hard several times to forcefully occupy the White House during the War of 1812. Even lit a match to it. So you can imagine the privilege I feel that I, a British subject, am finally taking up residence on behalf of my nation in this distinguished symbol of American democracy and resilient freedom . . . peacefully I might add! Or, so I hope, depending upon how our meetings unfold over the next several days. Remember that old saying: After a few days, fish and relatives in the same house began to smell. What about politicians?

Upon my arrival today, Franklin and his disarming wife Eleanor give me a brief tour of the White House.

Thankfully, we did not visit all of the rooms. If I remember correctly, I was told about thirty-five are bathrooms, eleven are bedrooms, three are kitchens, three are dining rooms, one a library, one a bowling alley, and one a movie theater. Twenty-eight rooms have fireplaces. The bathrooms seem disproportionally large in number to the rest of the house. I do wonder why so many commodes might be necessary in a house of government! I wonder if Roosevelt ever gets any privacy.

That reminds me of the time I was in the lavatory when the Lord Privy Seal came to see me. I told my trusted assistant, please tell the Lord Privy Seal that I am sealed in the privy and can only deal with one s*** at a time! Incidentally, the Lord Privy Seal is an honorable senior British cabinet minister who has no official duties. As a result of the lack of definition of responsibilities, the person holding the position can sometimes prove quite meddlesome.

Thanks to Eleanor's efforts, the Monroe Room on the second floor, which was her office, becomes quickly converted into a map room and office for my British delegation. Conveniently, it is across the hall from the Lincoln bedroom, which Henry Hopkins and his ten-year-old daughter occupy. He has not remarried since his wife died of cancer a few years ago. But there are rumors he dates.

In addition to requesting her office for my war room, I am afraid Eleanor and I get off on the wrong foot when I then tell her the bed in the room she has assigned me simply won't do. So I randomly wander the second floor and try out beds and pull out drawers. The Rose Bedroom, with its print scenes of Victorian England, makes me feel at home. I vaguely recall that Queen Elizabeth may have used this room during her visit to the U.S. in 1939. Eleanor looks exasperated but consents to my request to move.

I do confess that everything I have heard about Eleanor over the years causes me to admire her but I don't think I could live with her.

I also sense that she is a bit uneasy in my presence, but I don't take it personally since we both realize how so unlike we are by temperament.

Without any forewarning, though, she does me an enormous favor. As America's first lady, Eleanor has a clear sense of history and purpose. It becomes clear that she desperately hopes that her dear Franklin and I can work effectively together to save the free world. To that end, she shares with me what she has learned over many years of a long marriage. Rather abruptly, she says you must know that when Franklin uses the word *yes* it doesn't always mean he agrees. It simply means he's listening. I file this away in my memory bank and thank her for her candidness.

After arranging to move a half dozen heavily laden suitcases of mine to the Rose room, Mr. Fields, the White House butler, dutifully inquires about any other particular requirements I might have while a guest. Seeing this as a rare opportunity, I seize the opportunity and test his humor. I say to him we want to leave here as friends, right?

Well, then the best way to keep me happy is to "stock a tumbler of sherry in my room before breakfast, a couple of glasses of Scotch and soda before lunch, and French champagne and ninety-year-old brandy before I go to sleep at night."

Seeing that he doesn't flinch, I specify that he serve breakfast precisely at 9 a.m. with "something hot and something cold, two kinds of fresh fruit, and a pot of weak tea." To make it clearer, I add, "Something hot usually translates as eggs, bacon or ham, and toast. Something cold is usually two kinds of cold meat with English mustard and fruit. And for god's sake, don't forget the tumbler of sherry." Then I add please, no whistling. I don't care how happy it is, I hate whistling in the hallways. It disrupts my concentration. Then as if to answer my own question, I conclude, "I say, these requests seem most reasonable, don't you think?"

With a laugh, Mr. Fields replies, "Of course, Sir." Then with a straight face he asks that perhaps I would like President Roosevelt to join me every morning or should we keep this a secret? Franklin hasn't seen a breakfast like this since Eleanor, for health reasons, started overseeing his breakfast menu. It's been rather bland for him ever since. I prudently answer "secret," and Mr. Fields agrees for the sake of domestic tranquility.

To my delight, food is not yet rationed here, unlike at home. Since I do not believe in unnecessarily suffering as far as food is concerned, I let it be known my fondness for beef in every form. I am sooo very tired of eating wild game, fish, and root vegetables back in England.

The poor man takes my request far too seriously. I am sure this extravagance will not endear me to Mrs. Roosevelt.

Roosevelt

In honor of what she assumes to be a British tradition, Eleanor arranges to serve tea late in the afternoon on this first day of Churchill's arrival. However, in only a way that he can do it, Winston intimates that after ten hard, punishing days at sea, perhaps something stronger might soothe his soul.

Then he adds, "I have made it a rule of my life to never drink non-alcoholic drinks between meals."

So without much thought, I make a couple of Martinis, as is my custom, with two-thirds Plymouth gin, one-third dry vermouth. But after the first one, Churchill switches to Scotch and soda, specifying no more alcohol than a volume of mouthwash.

I suppose my dry martinis may be a little too sweet and rather meek by most standards . . . especially for Europeans. Churchill is a man who has trained hard over the years to hold his liquor. I must say I have been told that he has a large capacity. However, his request for small portions explains his capacity.

In honor of Churchill's arrival, I arranged to have the "Leo the Lion" skin rug that Ethiopia's Emperor Haile Selassie had given me placed in front of the bar to honor and welcome one of the last lions still bearing his fangs and roaring back at Hitler. Anyway, it proves a good conversation piece.

I am taking great pleasure in having Churchill as a guest in the house because his visit as a head of state dictates a departure from the drab White House meals we have been consuming over the years. Normally, at Eleanor's insistence, our menus are rather bland if not Spartan. She feels it important to send a signal that we eat no better than our citizens who have endured so much hardship throughout the Depression.

Churchill's visit has changed all that. The White House chef serves up a splendid meal of broiled chicken, potatoes, green beans, and leafy vegetables, followed by vanilla ice cream splashed with brandy.

In the presence of Lord Beaverbrook, Hopkins, Secretary of State Hull, and Foreign Secretary Lord Halifax, Winston and I spar lightly over dinner. Recalling that our Atlantic Charter meeting off the coast of Newfoundland leaked out to the press before I returned home, I kid him that the president of the United States can leave the country without getting permission from Congress. Therefore I submit that the leak must have come from the British side. In response, he laughs and then mutters that it must have been the women who spilled the beans. Of course, that doesn't go over particularly well with Eleanor and the other females at the table who sharply protest, supporting their British counterparts who they believe are naturally the more discrete of the two sexes.

We men adjourn to the Oval Office to talk a bit of business before calling it a night. Over stronger libations following dinner, Churchill becomes uncharacteristically quiet and contemplative. He says tonight is the first time in over a year he felt he could let his guard down. As a symbol of unwavering British confidence and bravery, in spite of his own personal anxieties, he has been elected to a position of enormous pressure to lead his people, while maintaining a stiff upper lip. Believe me, I empathize with him. Our jobs require that we do our best to suppress our nightmares in public.

With a hint of a tear in his eye, Winston begins sharing with us how terrifying the German blitz was from spring 1940 until spring 1941. Hitler believed that massive air raids, which killed forty-three thousand civilians, would intimidate London and Britain into surrendering. But, he says, Hitler was wrong. The bombings only solidified their resolve. In response to the blitz, their citizens were determined to "endure at all costs."

"London saw more than 450 raids between September and late December," Winston says. He adds that sometimes the bombs fell at the rate of one hundred per minute.

With the loss of thirty-six hundred civilians, December 29, 1940, brought the most devastating raid of all. Around 8 p.m., over two hundred German bombers hit London where it hurt most, the St. Paul's Cathedral area, the financial district, and the publishers and bookbinders community. The Germans dropped twenty-four thousand high-explosive bombs and one hundred thousand incendiary bombs that acted like Molotov cocktails as they fell to earth.

As a result, many thousands of fires raged throughout London for two days. The River Thames caught fire. Among the wasted and one-of-a-kind treasures: William the Conqueror's eleventh century charter granting London its freedom and eight of Christopher Wren's churches. Almost one-third of the city was laid to ruin.

As if to put an exclamation point on the matter, Winston describes inspecting, with his faithful wife Clementine by his side, the wreckage throughout London the next day. Together, they spread empathy and worked to forge community outrage into blades of steely resolve.

An old woman approached him on the street, asking when would the war end. Without a smile he told her, "When we have beaten them." He declared in the House of Commons, "We shall fight on the beaches, we shall fight on the landing grounds, we shall fight in the fields and in the streets, we shall fight in the hills; we shall never surrender."

Then, Winston pulls himself together and indicates he plans to sleep peacefully and soundly tonight with no thought of air raids.

Churchill

Perhaps it is the brandy or the Scotch but I lose my composure a bit after dinner tonight, reflecting on all the German air raids and their indiscriminate destruction.

I inform Franklin of the priceless treasures that perished and what we did after the initial bombings to protect our remaining artistic and cultural heritage. We moved our precious Magna Carta, dating back to 1215, to tunnels bored deep into protective hill sites in Wales, along with other priceless documents and art.

The Fifth Amendment to the U.S. Constitution, that "no person shall be deprived of life, liberty, or property" without a due process, descends directly from the British Magna Carta. We knew that Hitler detested such public freedoms and would try to destroy the historically rare document given the chance.

I tell Franklin that we continue to receive reports throughout Europe of Nazis looting national treasures on an incomprehensible scale and transporting them back to Germany. In particular, they have targeted and seized private property from Jewish people in their country and now elsewhere. What they can't steal they often destroy.

Under these circumstances, I advise him that his own government should place a high priority on securing its own national treasures as quickly as possible. Our enemies would love to vandalize symbols of America's heritage too.

Franklin replies he has not yet had much time to think about or digest this new threat. With a scowl written across his face, he responds that destroying works of art, sculpture, buildings, monuments, music, and books represents a heinous assault on a nation's history, identity, and culture. He promises he will urgently act on my information first thing in the morning.

Before going to bed, I anxiously ask if Franklin believes his government will stick to a European-first strategy in preference to striking out against Imperial Japan. He responds that he thinks they will but it is still subject to congressional approval. I feel encouraged; that what I fear the most seems less likely. Since I have been asked to formally address Congress the day after Christmas, it also means that it remains terribly important that I personally win their favor on this most important matter.

We also discuss the general situation in Europe. I emphasize that I thought North Africa should become our first major and joint war priority . . . where we can make the Axis bleed. Following victory there, we could secure the Mediterranean and mount a push up through Italy and onward. Roosevelt seems to agree with this assessment.

We finish the evening reviewing the draft of a declaration regarding our joint intentions, including the provision that "no power would make peace without agreement from associate powers."

Just as we decide to call it a day around midnight, we receive troubling news that Japan has launched a major offensive in the Philippines. The stakes immediately go up, and now I hope that the U.S. will not knee-jerk and lose sight of their focus on Europe and North Africa.

St. Paul's Cathedral area in flames following Nazi air raids.
By *Daily Mail* photographer Herbert Mason from Fleet Street
on the night of December 29, 1940. *U.S. National Archives*

The USS *Shaw* burns during the Pearl Harbor attack.
U.S. National Archives

The USS *Downes* (left) and USS *Cassin* at Pearl Harbor.
U.S. Navy History and Heritage Command

The repaired USS *Helena* in June 1942, six months after being
torpedoed at Pearl Harbor. The author's uncle, Captain Jim
Baird, was on board at the time of the attack. *Licensed under
public domain via Wikimedia Commons*

Chapter Three

THE FRIENDLY WHITE HOUSE OCCUPATION

December 23, 1941

Churchill

This morning, Mr. Fields surprises me with two trays of food . . . one full of cold choices and the other hot . . . enough for three people. On a very full stomach, almost to the point of aching, I think afterward that I have gone too far in expressing my wishes. I promise later in the day to make amends with Mr. Fields.

By custom, neither Roosevelt nor I exactly roll out of bed at the crack of dawn. But in the White House, our habits are clearly different. I usually stay up until around 2 a.m. sipping on a nightcap, enjoying a cigar, and brooding over my map tables. While most slumber, I follow in the various time zones the progression of the war throughout Europe, Africa, and Asia. I receive a steady flow of updates from our commanders and cabinet members.

When they request my input, I do my best to discern an appropriate reply but often with reservation, and even trepidation. I recognize that there is often no better judge of which course to take than those who are planted on the battlefield. And, I ask myself is this request for my input strategic or tactical in nature? Now that I am older, and questionably wiser, I worry about crippling my people by exercising too much personal involvement.

Unfortunately, over the years I have learned that war does not dictate who is right, only who remains still standing on the battlefield. I know that while they are not always correct, situations call for decisiveness. And if I didn't lose sleep over them, I'd be subhuman and too detached to effectively lead. I must agree with my wife that when it comes to momentous decisions, a clear conscience on them signals a very fuzzy memory . . . especially when hundreds and thousands of lives are at stake.

In contrast to my nocturnal habits, poor Franklin remains saddled like a burro under the tight rein of Eleanor's disciplined hand. She shepherds him to bed early to conserve his stamina, which the lingering effects of polio continue to undermine. Like me he is on call twenty-four hours a day seven days a week. And, it is not unusual for his staff to awaken him in the middle of the night for instruction on this matter or that.

The previous evening, my first in the White House, Harry Hopkins, an inveterate night owl, wandered across the hallway from his residence in the Lincoln room and knocked on the door to join me for a nightcap in the Madison Room. Since his visit earlier in the year to London, our trust, friendship, and ease of communicating frankly with one another has steadily grown along with my admiration for him.

He knows and shares my late-evening meandering ways. Before his first visit, I learned from M15, my secret service agency, that in his prime Hopkins partied, caroused, flirted, and night-owled with unparalleled stamina. Now his health is fragile and what stamina remains is like a single ray of light streaming through a magnifying glass, devoted and concentrated, like his boss, on defeating our common enemies. However, he retains a sense of humor and a sarcastic wit. And a pretty girl passing by can still momentarily catch his eye and distract his attention.

On entering, the first thing that catches Harry's view are my map tables displaying war zones, likely future engagements, and troop and naval positions, including risk assessments. Harry says that Roosevelt has nothing like these in the White House. He immediately perceives the advantage of installing something similar to improve communications between Roosevelt, his cabinet, and the many generals and admirals with whom they will be communicating with in Washington and around the world.

I ask Harry if he ever met Hitler personally. Harry replies that his only firsthand observation was at the 1936 Olympics in Berlin. He recalls how distraught Hitler looked when the American Jesse Owens, a black athlete of extraordinary talent, won four gold medals. In disgust and with a clear racial bias, Hitler fled the stadium without any acknowledgement of Owens' unprecedented accomplishment.

Then, Harry inquires if I ever met Hitler.

I respond that there were two opportunities. Regarding the first one, I profoundly regret not taking the opportunity to kill him, whatever the cost to me personally. Unknown to either of us at the time, in 1916 we were both fighting in the front lines, dug down in trenches separated by no more than forty to fifty meters. He was then a corporal and I was a major with almost one thousand troops under my command. We shelled, shot, gassed, and bayoneted one another senseless to appease our politicians and senior commanders.

Digressing for a moment, I blurt out that bloody slaughter between enemies at such close quarters remains indelibly and emotionally imprinted in my memory. My men suffered trench foot, crawled on their own feces, lived among the rats feeding on our crumbs, slept among the dead and decaying corpses, and were as likely to die of disease, or wither from insanity, than succumb from battle. Never has my leadership been so severely tested as it was in that damp, sodden subterranean hellhole. The agonizing screams from the wounded on both sides still echo in my ears and haunt me yet today.

In my dual role as prime minister and minister of defense, I'll do whatever I can today to minimize these sorts of direct and prolonged engagements where enemies gain little strategic ground at great human sacrifice. Thus, I strongly prefer to wear down the Axis powers by air and sea, strangling their infrastructure and political will to support warfare.

The second time, Hitler courted me and other European leaders shortly after he came to power in 1933. He wished to discuss with us the depression then occurring in our respective countries. He wanted to explain how Germany needed to rebuild its industrial base to create jobs, never mentioning the focus on weapons of warfare.

I told the German ambassador that I would be happy to meet with Hitler, but before I did I wanted to know more clearly his position since writing *Mein Kampf.* Had it softened or changed? I did not pull any punches and explained to the ambassador that I found Hitler's expressed hatred of Jews, communists, socialists, and the weak deeply disturbing and perhaps an ominous foretelling of the future. I was already hearing appalling rumors. I never heard back from him nor did I think I would. He probably knew that some of my best friends were Jews, as were my father's friends.

I ask Harry if he remembers Hitler's campaign promise to his people regarding their future prosperity. He thinks for a moment and guesses: Wasn't it something like "give me five years and you will not recognize the face of Germany again"?

Correct. With the mighty armies of Britain, the U.S., and Russia united, let's make Hitler's dream come true in ways that he could never have dreamed or imagined!

Roosevelt

On Churchill's first morning here, it is a bone-chilling day in D.C. As a result of the Depression, we, the government, have postponed badly needed repairs to the White House for more than ten years. Such an undertaking is just not politically prudent or advisable when so many people lost their homes during the Depression or still dwell in poverty.

So we turn up the boilers to compensate for the drafts and energy leaking from the walls, sagging floors, and warping windows. Nevertheless, the old girl still has good bones and certainly curb appeal. But another five years of postponing repairs could ruin the Grande Dame. Now that we are at war on two fronts, the state of the building remains the least of my concerns.

Churchill wakes midmorning, as is his custom, and lights the first of the seven to ten Cuban cigars he devours each day. He brandishes them in his chubby hand as if he were a symphony conductor directing an attentive orchestra.

He begins the day with the first of two long, hot soaks in the tub, probably to offset the chill in the house. I envision him lounging in water up to his neck, with steam and cigar smoke merging around him. He probably doesn't bother with an ashtray, flicking ashes into the water. Following what he calls his therapeutic bath, he consumes a large breakfast. Three hours later he announces he is getting hungry for lunch.

We discover that Churchill's enormous work ethic matches his appetite . . . day and night. His high energy level burns like a freight train, fueled by cigars, calories, and liquor. He appears to possess the stamina of a man half his age.

Churchill

On my first full day in the White House, I explore the grounds alone before lunch. The views in all directions are stunning and by looking at surrounding buildings and monuments, I gain a sense of this nation's untapped raw power. I consider it my sacred mission and Lord Beaverbrook's to help Franklin mobilize America into one galvanized effort to win the war.

Exposing me to his traditional approach to lunch, Franklin and I crack cold lobster over his trinket-strewn desk. Soon we have shells and mayonnaise sauce scattered across the top of his desk and surrounding documents. Stinking of lobster and sauce, outgoing communiqués and memorandums will probably tattle on our escapades. Both satisfied, neither of us gives the mess a second thought.

In fact, a mess seems like the natural order of things. Franklin's relaxed Oval Office is full of junk, half-opened parcels, books and papers, and whimsical souvenirs along with his stamp collection piled everywhere. A more orderly, perhaps less creatively minded person might find it distracting, but he seems a man at peace with his environment.

At lunch, Franklin mentions that Hopkins has informed him of my war maps, codes, charts, and statistics spread across the Monroe Room walls and tabletops. He requests to see them since they might serve as a model for one he thinks he should install in an adjacent room.

With a twinkle in his eye, he says that Harry shared with him that we had been up until 2 a.m. smoking Cuban Romero y Julietta cigars, swirling and swigging Hine brandy, and discussing political events.

He also mentions he learned that Harry and I shared a few ribald stories that Eleanor would not approve of but he would!

Franklin particularly likes the story I told Hopkins about the sanctimonious Methodist bishop I sat next to at a reception in Canada. When the waitress offered him a sherry, the bishop blurted out that he would rather commit adultery than take an intoxicating drink. In response to this rather sobering comment, I said to the cheerful young lady trying to do her best, "Miss, come back. I didn't know we had a choice!" She of course knew I didn't mean it, but she giggled at my retaliation. The bishop and I had little to say to one another the rest of the evening. The fact that Franklin liked the story revealed that he has a sense of humor and certainly isn't a prude. We are going to get along just fine.

Franklin makes a point that he doesn't want to be left out of future strategic late-night sessions, whatever their nature, and this coming evening he'd welcome a personal tour of my map room. Smiling, I tell him it would be my pleasure to host such an event in his own home. In the evenings, I suspect things have been rather dull for Franklin, and an adventure with the boys might spice up his life.

In the afternoon we take our first joint press conference. As we enter what's called the press closet, he says the "wolves are about to join us in sheep's clothing!" The room is stuffed with reporters and photographers and it wreaks of smoke, whiskey, dust, and sweat from frequent and hard use. Anything with wood sports cigarette burns. As I begin to speak, Franklin shouts out, "Winston, they can't see you," so I step up on a chair. With his encouragement, they pepper me with questions. He sits back smiling at the spectacle of a very portly head of state balancing himself rather tenuously on a chair to speak to a willing and friendly audience.

One reporter asks me if the key to victory against Japan will depend on how we tackle Singapore. This question opens the door for me to register why I came to America. I say, "No, the key is the resolute manner in which the British and American democracies throw themselves into the conflict." I then add that over the next couple of weeks together, our mutual staffs will meet extensively on just this subject. The results of these strategic discussions and the order of military engagements will largely govern how fast and effectively we defeat the Nazis' and the Imperial Japanese armies.

Following our meeting with the press, Franklin and I hold our first joint meeting with our respective chiefs of staff. Truthfully, despite high expectations, this meeting does not go well. First, Roosevelt contradicts the agreement I thought we had the night before. He backs off preparations to focus on a North African victory in 1942 by saying that might not be possible until 1944. We accomplish very little and no other specific proposals emerge from our joint chiefs of staffs.

It becomes very clear that both sides seriously disagree over how to go about prosecuting the war. For instance, General George Marshall once again makes it clear, as he did in Newfoundland, that he thinks it is naive of the British to believe that we can defeat Germany in any other way short of a direct land invasion of the European mainland. Sadly, he says that means another brutalizing drive to Berlin, just like in 1918 to end World War I. This is the approach I hope with all my heart to avoid. I determine to persuade everyone of the error in their thinking before I leave Washington.

To make matters worse, the Americans lack any clear idea yet as to their abilities to produce weapons on a mass scale. They have not yet projected how long it will take them to construct a modern-day army, navy, and air force. Unlike us, none of these three branches of service appear to collaborate or work very closely with one another. Strategically, there's little integration. The situation frustrates my British colleagues. But, I am optimistic it's not insurmountable.

Behind closed doors, Franklin and I privately discuss that we need to help change and guide perceptions before our respective staffs become solidified in their thinking and antagonistic toward one another. Candidly, he acknowledges that his chiefs of staffs think mine are arrogant know-it-alls. They harbor the belief that our only interest is to get as much equipment and fighting men as we can get our hands on without Americans participating in decisions as to how these collective resources will be deployed.

Equally blunt, I tell Franklin that my chiefs think the Americans behave bureaucratically, demonstrate disorganization, are burdened by inter-service rivalries, and seem ignorant of the terrifying realities of modern-day warfare. They perceive that the Americans still reel from the surprise and aftershock of Japan's massive invasions throughout the Pacific region a little over two weeks ago. Consequently they think the Americans, perhaps understandably so, have yet to collect their thoughts on how to proceed to harness their inherent industry and military power into a potent fighting force.

Happy hour comes none too soon following the debacle from our first joint meeting. In the evening, Franklin, several of his guests, and I assemble for drinks in the Red Room before dinner. We both consider the cocktail hour a sacred and inviolate event.

While Franklin is very fond of what he calls Martinis, I am not. As a new guest in his house, I am not bold enough to register my disdain. Each of his concoctions, which he calls an art form, strike me as different experiments with rum, gin, vermouth, and fruit juice. With great gusto, he shakes the mix vigorously over ice to chill it. Then he graciously and ceremoniously pours the brew, without a dribble, into glasses all lined up in formation like new military inductees awaiting their orders. With an audible sigh of approval, Franklin marvels at his liquid masterpieces and then dispatches them onto his guests.

When Franklin graciously refills my glass before I can decline, I excuse myself as quickly and politely as possible to go to the nearest bathroom . . . something we older men do a lot. Then I toss his godawful drink down the drain. To fake it, I plunk the olives back in the glass and add water. In the White House, I've already found that the drinks are too hard and the toilet paper's too soft.

Franklin and Eleanor know that two years at war make beef a luxury reserved for the British fighting soldiers and sailors. We ration it for civilians. I have always been a voracious beef eater and quite fond of it. Imagine my surprise and delight when a magnificent prime rib arrives for dinner. I mentally salivate! Brandishing knife and fork Franklin, with a gleam in his eye, skillfully carves the roast and ceremoniously serves each plate. From the broad smile on his face, I detect it has been quite a while since he has eaten beef thanks to Eleanor's frugal Depression mentality regarding self-sacrifice. She is definitely an idealist and, like her husband, possesses astute political instincts that manifest themselves even at their dinner table.

Franklin and I devour the beef like starving wolves. Pouring on the praises, he claims he has never eaten a better serving of meat and speculates that corn feeding cattle contributes to the flavor. My only thought is how tender each bite is compared to our old milk cows that retire to the British butcher shops when they can longer produce milk. They're tough on the gums.

Over dinner and several glasses of wine, Franklin and I debate the Boer War in South Africa. The Boers first rose up against their British masters in 1880 and then again in 1899. While at Harvard, Franklin supported these European settlers' position and claims to self-rule. I participated in the second Boer War as a British correspondent, military observer, and prisoner. After my miraculous escape, the Boers placed a large bounty on my head, either dead or alive.

We reach a friendly stalemate on our differing views . . . a prelude I am sure of harder discussions and negotiations over the next several days. More importantly, I think our little tit for tat indicates how easily the two of us can work together on critical issues that need addressing and, when necessary, politely agree to disagree.

To my surprise, a relaxed Franklin volunteers that he experienced some disappointments while at Harvard. He expressed regret that he had not been as popular or successful as he would like to have been, even though he served as editor of the student newspaper.

From such a proud man, this is an extraordinarily honest admission about his youth. It tells me that he feels comfortable and at ease in my presence.

For a brief moment, I mull over his comment, take a long puff on my cigar, and then growl: "When I hear a man say that his childhood and youth were the happiest times of his life, I think he has led a pretty poor life." This response elicits a deep chuckle from Franklin, who clearly appreciates the indirect compliment.

Roosevelt

I suggest to Winston that on Christmas Eve we should jointly speak to our respective citizens to convey our mutual hope for the future, shared convictions, and unbreakable solidarity. He agrees and we spend part of the afternoon drafting these messages and comparing notes.

In the early evening we begin to conduct our second meeting with our respective military leaders and key staff members, hoping to create the trust and cooperation we will be asking them to mirror. To get off on the right foot after the last debacle, we decide that the initial order of business to break the ice should be to determine what to call ourselves. Seems simple enough. If we can find agreement on this matter, perhaps it will set the stage for resolving more serious discussions to follow.

For the sake of history, we decide we need a prominent name for what we hope will be a landscaping change of meetings over the next week or two. After much good-natured haggling, brainstorming, and even dark humor, the formal code name we decide upon for our secret meetings in the White House and about the capital is Arcadia. For a few brief moments we considered calling it Operation Proctology!

Arcadia means "adventuresome" in Latin but "pastoral" in Greek. I personally like the name because Washington seems like a paradise compared to London's prolonged wartime footing.

But, one of the senior British officers volunteers that he is familiar with the term *Arcadia* and understands a different definition. He says people with this name tend, like the mythical figure Zeus, to possess powerful personalities, initiate events, and like to lead rather than follow. He adds that they are goal driven and determined. They implement their ideas with efficiency, sometimes aggressively. As unique, creative individuals, they may resent bureaucratic authority and are sometimes stubborn, proud, and impatient.

Although we have no time or even desire to validate the veracity of what he says, the officer's description wins the day for both our code name and the virtues we as allies jointly wish to call upon to press the war against the Germans, Japanese, and Italians.

Unfortunately, agreeing on a name to call our conferences turns out to be the only thing we accomplish today! Winston and I are again disappointed that the bonding of minds and forces between our military leaders fails to gel the way we envision. We conclude that we need to rethink how best to go about setting the stage for further cooperation. Then, we once again surrender to the beckoning cocktail hour to gain some relief from the tensions and bickering in the room.

Whenever I can, I gently surface the topic of British imperialism with Churchill and needle him about it. He opens the window when he brings up the subject of how he escaped being captured by the Boers over dinner. I recall that following that escapade he wrote a book about the experience and went on a lecture tour.

I say, "Didn't Samuel Clemens (Mark Twain) introduce you at the Waldorf Astoria to a New York City audience back in 1900?" Of course he did. I add that I recall Clemens roasted him a bit about British global imperialism in his introduction. Churchill chimes in and says he also criticized Americans about their own version of imperialism and domain over Puerto Rico, the Panama Zone, Hawaii, Guam, and the Philippines.

Churchill remembers how vehemently Clemens disapproved of the war in South Africa. At the time Clemens thought that England sinned when she fought the Boers and the United States was sinning by meddling in the affairs of the Filipinos. He said something like, "England and America were kin in almost everything; now they are kin in sin." But Churchill adds that Clemens encouraged bonds of friendship between England and America. And thanks to his efforts, our countries have remained on good terms ever since, and that's what brings us together tonight.

So Churchill adroitly dodges my little dig. But, Clemens was right about the Philippines. My fifth cousin Theodore Roosevelt, also my wife's uncle, had serious imperialistic intentions and wanted to use the Philippines to establish a major presence in the Far East. We were wrong to be there, and almost 250,000 Filipinos lost their lives resisting our governance . . . a sad and little remembered time in our nation's history. Fortunately, after we abandoned our claims the Filipinos became good friends. The whole affair explains why, among other reasons, I disdain imperialism and would like to see an end to it everywhere.

And it still haunts me yet today, in the light of Pearl Harbor, that my cousin Teddy may have unwittingly set the stage for Japanese imperialism. During his presidency he invited and encouraged Japan to create their version of our Monroe Doctrine dating back to President James Monroe in 1823.

The doctrine made us the big brother for all of the Americas. It essentially stated that if any European countries intervened in the politics of North, Central, or South America, then the U.S. may perceive such action as a hostile act against U.S. interests. My well-intentioned cousin suggested that Japan, as Asia's most advanced country, should step into that leadership role on behalf of their less developed neighbors like China and Korea. I am sure he never dreamed that exposing Japan to the concepts of the Monroe Doctrine would lead to them enslaving other countries. As a Roosevelt, I feel personally obliged to clean up this mess.

Churchill

Making good on his promise, Franklin joins me late into the evening to talk politics, history, war preparations, and love of the navy.

We are both proud of the Atlantic Charter, which we coauthored in Newfoundland on board ship. We spend some time reflecting upon the importance of this document in setting the stage for future world affairs as soon as we defeat Germany and Japan. The charter champions the concepts of self-determination, freedom of the seas, and the improvement of working and living conditions for all people.

Roosevelt has been particularly insistent on inserting language leading to an end to colonialism. I was not willing to use this word and so we compromised, substituting "self-determination" for "an end to colonialism."

I refuse to go down in history as becoming the first prime minister to concede to the dismantling of the British Empire. We view ourselves as defenders of minorities in nations that are not ready for self-government . . . especially India where Muslims and Hindus do not get along, not to mention a caste system that treats those at the bottom like dogs.

When Eleanor challenged me earlier on the matter, I said, "Are we talking about the brown-skinned Indians in India who have prospered under British rule or the red-skinned Indians in America who are now almost extinct?"

Looking toward the Middle East, I tell Franklin they are just as fractured. I point out that this region is highly pluralistic. Shiites, Sunnis, Kurds, Christians, Druze, and various tribes have been held together for centuries by iron-fisted kings, dictators, or colonial powers. Until these various groups can learn to respect their diversities, they will struggle to develop sustainable institutions for self-government and shared prosperities.

As evidence, I explain that forty-two years ago while a young soldier and journalist covering the River War in the Sudan, I formed some very strong opinions from firsthand experiences with extremists of the Islamic faith. And here in the modern age of 1941, nothing leads me to believe anything has changed. Then as now, wherever extremist followers of the Prophet rule, property ownership is fragile and insecure. Every woman belongs to a man as his absolute property. Slavery is pervasive and brutal. Life is cheap. Fundamentalist believers paralyze social development and are extremely militant. And, where they have proselytized their twisted beliefs in Central Africa, it has raised fearless warriors at every step.

As a matter of fact, I distrust extremists of any faith for their desire to impose their will and intolerant beliefs on others.

To lighten up the conversation, I jokingly observe that Franklin and I are so much alike in how we play the political game of chess with world events.

Franklin knows that the charter will be more palatable to members of Congress whose memories still remain sharp regarding the colonial thumb the British had on America during its infancy. We both hope that a reference to self-determination will appease Congress for the time being.

To placate Franklin, I reluctantly agree to send Sir Stafford Cripps, an outspoken Labour Party critic of British Colonial rule, to India early next year to offer a proposal for postwar independence. He laughs and says he also understood that I wanted the charter signed because it brought the U.S. a big step closer to aligning with the British in the war against Germany and Italy. I confirm this and tell him that by the time we met in Newfoundland, I had already become privately convinced that there was no way that Britain could win the war without full participation from the United States.

We end the evening talking about our dysfunctional first joint staff meetings and what to do about it. We both pledge to encourage our chiefs of staffs to set aside any lingering prejudices, seek help and advice from the other, admit weaknesses where they exist, share knowledge and experience, and listen better to each other.

We also think it might be a good idea to begin individual chiefs of staff meetings by function . . . the navy meeting with the navy, and so forth. This might help them focus, discover common ground, and hopefully begin to forge some friendships, especially after hours.

Roosevelt

I must say this was a fun, stimulating evening spent with Churchill. He is much more of a student of history than I am and more inclined to read the world's great literary masterpieces. Not that I don't enjoy either one, but my polio has somewhat diminished my stamina for long hours of reading while sitting still in a chair. And, my political responsibilities now keep me focused on contemporary news and events.

I joke that his sense and knowledge of history is so vast that he should someday write a history of the British Empire. To my surprise he says he had already started on it, beginning in 1937 while he was out of politics.

The title he has in mind suggests how ambitious his undertaking is: *A History of the English-Speaking Peoples*. Winston has already made considerable progress, covering the period from Caesar's invasion of Britain through Viking occupations and all the way to the beginning of the First World War. At that stage in the book, he was recalled to political duty. He put it aside for government service, first as admiral of the Royal Navy and shortly thereafter as prime minister.

Then with a chuckle, Winston says, "History will prove kind to me, for I intend to continue writing it!"

Clearly Winston draws upon his profound understanding of the past as the key to understanding the present and framing the future. He says he believes that "the longer you look back, the further you can look forward." I think this is one of the reasons he saw where Hitler and Germany were headed before almost anyone else.

It is well past 2 a.m. when both of our bodies feel compelled to surrender to some rest and recuperation to face Christmas Eve day more sober than we are now. Our relationship has grown to the point that Winston insists on pushing my wheelchair to the elevator and up to my room. As you might imagine, the journey is a rather wobbly one but he accomplishes the feat. Mr. Fields, the White House butler, helps me into bed.

Before turning off the lights, I extract a promise from Fields that he will tell not a soul how late the evening was and especially not Eleanor, who sleeps in a separate bedroom . . . which is another story.

December 24, 1941

Churchill

Last evening we strategized, "whiskeyed," and smoked late into the night. For humanitarian reasons, I congratulated Franklin on repealing Prohibition. He smiled and said that he thought a winning campaign slogan for the 1932 run at the presidency might have been along the lines of "Provide a bottle and a glass and I'll end the recession and get America off its ass!" We both laughed.

We were quite a pair, exchanging political adventures and ideas and blowing tobacco smoke for hours on end. Whenever he grins, Franklin's long cigarette holder, which he addictively clinches between his teeth, launches upward. Very aristocratic.

He seemed to enjoy my own night-owlish habits. Repeatedly, I hinted that perhaps it was way past his customary bedtime. He brushed me off with the comment that we had so much to accomplish and so little time to do it together. Truth be known, I think he likes defying Eleanor, who since my arrival fusses constantly over his state of health.

We both awake midmorning, and I spend the time until lunch reviewing and responding to cable messages on the home and war front.

In the afternoon, I diligently work on the message I plan to deliver to the U.S. Congress the day after Christmas. For a lot of reasons, this could be the most important speech that I have ever had to prepare. It is essential to Britain's survival that the U.S. goes to war simultaneously on both fronts, but with most of the immediate emphasis on Europe first, followed by Japan. We need their physical presence as soon as possible as well as assurances that they will continue to help supplement us with arms and other essential military equipment.

Also this afternoon, Franklin continues to prepare and polish his address to the nation. He plans to deliver his message later in the evening, along with lighting the National Christmas Tree on the White House balcony. He invites me to review his speech. Upon reading it, I conclude how very appropriate it is for addressing a nation in shock and outrage. Then to my surprise, he also asks me to make a few comments to his people and to join him in lighting the ceremonial tree . . . something I am sure no other foreign head of state has ever done. Long-ago enemies have now become friends. As they lie in their graves, I briefly ponder what King George III and President Washington think of that!

Roosevelt

It is very special to have Winston join me on my radio broadcast to the nation. Early in the cold evening twilight, a crowd of twenty thousand people gathers on the White House lawn along with several hundred reporters. A crescent moon shines above us. To the south looms the Washington Monument as we watch the sun dip behind the Virginia hills.

Standing on the balcony, I solemnly lead off with my speech...feeling much like the reassuring father of an apprehensive nation. It is being broadcast around the world. I begin ...

Fellow workers for freedom:

There are many men and women in America—sincere and faithful men and women—who are asking themselves this Christmas:

How can we light our trees? How can we give our gifts?

How can we meet and worship with love and with uplifted spirit and heart in a world at war, a world of fighting and suffering and death?

How can we pause, even for a day, even for Christmas Day, in our urgent labor of arming a decent humanity against the enemies which beset it?

How can we put the world aside, as men and women put the world aside in peaceful years, to rejoice in the birth of Christ?

These are natural—inevitable—questions in every part of the world, which is resisting the evils emanating from Japan, Germany, and Italy.

And even as we ask these questions, we know the answer. There is another preparation demanded of this nation beyond and beside the preparation of weapons and materials of war.

There is demanded also of us the preparation of our hearts; the arming of our hearts. And when we make ready our hearts for the labor and the suffering and the ultimate victory, which lie ahead, then we observe Christmas Day—with all of its memories and all of its meanings—as we should.

Looking into the days to come, I have set aside a day of prayer and in that proclamation I have said:

The year 1941 has brought upon our nation a war of aggression by powers dominated by arrogant rulers whose selfish purpose is to destroy free institutions. They would thereby take from the freedom-loving peoples of the earth the hard-won liberties gained over many centuries.

The new year of 1942 calls for the courage and the resolution of old and young to help to win a world struggle in order that we may preserve all we hold dear.

We are confident in our devotion to country, in our love of freedom, in our inheritance of courage. But our strength, as the strength of all men everywhere, is of greater avail as God upholds us.

Therefore, I do hereby appoint the first day of the year 1942 as a day of prayer, of asking forgiveness for our shortcomings of the past, of consecration to the tasks of the present, of asking God's help in days to come.

We need His guidance that this people may be humble in spirit but strong in the conviction of the right; steadfast to endure sacrifice, and brave to achieve a victory of liberty and peace.

Our strongest weapon in this war is that conviction of the dignity and brotherhood of man which Christmas Day signifies—more than any other day or any other symbol.

Against enemies who preach the principles of hate and practice them, we set our faith in human love and in God's care for us and all men everywhere.

It is in that spirit, and with particular thoughtfulness of those, our sons and brothers, who serve in our armed forces on land and sea, near and far—those who serve and endure for us—that we light our Christmas candles now across the continent from one coast to the other on this Christmas Eve.

We have joined with many other nations and peoples in a very great cause. Millions of them have been engaged in the task of defending good with their life-blood for months and for years.

One of their great leaders stands beside me. He and his people in many parts of the world are having their Christmas trees with their little children around them, just as we do here. He and his people have pointed the way in courage and in sacrifice for the sake of little children everywhere.

And so I am asking tonight my associate, my old and good

friend, Winston Churchill, prime minister of Great Britain, to say a word to the people of America, old and young.

Churchill

Franklin gives me the most gracious introduction ever. I am elated and encouraged by how much progress our personal relationship has made since our meeting in Newfoundland last August.

Tonight he introduces me as a friend that he might have known all his life. With that touching gesture, he passes the microphone to me and I clear my voice and begin:

> I spend this anniversary and festival far from my country, far from my family, yet I cannot truthfully say that I feel far from home. Whether it be the ties of blood on my mother's side, or the friendships I have developed here over many years of active life, or the commanding sentiment of comradeship in the common cause of great peoples who speak the same language, who kneel at the same altars, and, to a very large extent, pursue the same ideals, I cannot feel myself a stranger here in the center and at the summit of the United States.
>
> I feel a sense of unity and fraternal association which, added to the kindliness of your welcome, convinces me that I have a right to sit at your fireside and share your Christmas joys.
>
> This is a strange Christmas Eve. Almost the whole world is locked in deadly struggle, and, with the most terrible weapons which science can devise, the nations advance upon each other. Ill would it be for us this Christmastide if we were not sure that no greed for the land or wealth of any other people, no vulgar ambition, no morbid lust for material gain at the expense of others, had led us to the field.
>
> Here, in the midst of war, raging and roaring over all the lands and seas, creeping nearer to our hearts and homes, here, amid all the tumult, we have tonight the peace of the spirit in each cottage home and in every generous heart. Therefore we may cast aside for this night at least the cares and dangers which beset us, and make for the children an evening of happiness in a world of storm. Here, then, for one night only, each home throughout

the English-speaking world should be a brightly lighted island of happiness and peace.

Let the children have their night of fun and laughter. Let the gifts of Father Christmas delight their play. Let us grown-ups share to the full in their unstinted pleasures before we turn again to the stern task and the formidable years that lie before us, resolved that, by our sacrifice and daring, these same children shall not be robbed of their inheritance or denied their right to live in a free and decent world.

And so, in God's mercy, a happy Christmas to you all.

Roosevelt

I am deeply touched by Churchill's Christmas Eve address. It flows with emotion that can only come from one who has witnessed great tragedy and loss and paid the highest of sacrifices. I look inward and think very soon I will be wearing and walking in a very similar pair of shoes once our young men and women come face to face with our enemies.

Following our speeches, we jointly light the National Christmas Tree . . . the kind of pageantry that Winston clearly loves. Then, at Eleanor's prearrangement, the Marine Band performs "Joy to the World" and "Hallelujah Chorus" from Handel's "Messiah."

After the public ceremony, we return to the White House for a Roosevelt family tradition. Available grandchildren and family gather round to decorate and light our own tree in the grand ceremonial East Room. Once they finish, Eleanor hands me an 1866 publication of Charles Dickens' *A Christmas Carol*. This edition has belonged to several generations of the Roosevelt family. As the current heir, it is my responsibility to inject great drama and flair into relating the tale. I invite Winston to sit beside me as I read from the book. To my delight, he occasionally joins me, reciting verses from memory . . . with equal drama! The youngsters delight in our Dickens Duet and the adults are very amused, as am I.

Later that evening Winston returns to work in the Monroe Room, polishing his speech to Congress for December 26. Encountering him in the hallway, Winston asks Harry if he and Diana Hopkins, his nine-year-old daughter, could come to his room.

When Harry arrives he finds Winston comfortably dressed in his favorite red velvet siren suit, a garment he designed himself "with a zip all-in-one that his children referred to as his rompers." It allows him to quickly dress at the sound of an air raid siren. Although Winston adores and wears a wide variety of military uniforms, he favors, considering his substantial girth, this comfortable and relaxed-fitting non-uniform.

Winston has never been away from his darling wife Clementine, their four children, and their grandchildren on Christmas, and he feels sentimental.

A very nervous nine-year-old is ushered into the prime minister's room. As she approaches, he snuffs out his cigar and then holds out his arms and embraces the awestruck Diana, saying, "I'm a lonely old father and grandfather on Christmas Eve and I want a little girl to hug." This little girl, so secure in his arms, represents to him the worthiness of the cause that has been consuming his life day and night for the last couple of years.

Winston shows Diana a picture of his young grandson sitting on the floor with him. Shyly, Diana perceptively observes how much his grandson resembles him. He laughs and says, "That's kind of you, Diana, but the truth is, with my round face, smooth pink skin, and bald head, I resemble every baby!" This disarms Diana and they both giggle.

December 25, 1941

Churchill

Franklin advised me last evening not to work my long hours into the night because we would rise earlier than usual to attend a Christmas morning church service.

We both appreciate the majesty and symbolism of public worship in contrast to the pagan fascism of Hitler's regime.

But, Franklin is much more of a faithful churchman than I. I tell him I definitely believe in God but that I am more like a "flying buttress who supports the church from the outside!"

Of course, much of the reason I don't often attend church on Sunday mornings, or any morning for that matter, has to do with my natural body cycle. By custom I work late into the night, when I am at my most creative.

Our first worship together was actually on the HMS *Prince of Wales* when we were in Newfoundland. We discovered that we were both reared in a similar Anglican faith, and familiar with most of the great old Anglo-Saxon and American hymns. The worship service I organized on board the *Prince of Wales* included such grand hymns as "Onward Christian Soldiers," "Oh God Our Help in Ages Past," and "Eternal Father Strong to Save."

At our service at sea, I honestly wept and remembered it as a great hour to have lived. Franklin confessed to me later that singing "Onward Christian Soldiers" together cemented for him the future of our relationship.

Roosevelt

I take Winston to the Foundry Methodist Church, which is about a mile from the White House. I like to sing hymns with the "Methodies" despite being an Episcopalian. Army Chief of Staff George Marshall and Vice President Henry Wallace join us. We all sing loudly with great gusto, if not exactly in tune.

This Christmas morning, the minister prays for "those who are dying on land and sea" in defense of our country. Certainly, his message fortifies the "faith of all who believe in the moral governance of the universe."

To my surprise, this is the first time Churchill has ever heard sung "O Little Town of Bethlehem," which was written by a Philadelphia pastor while visiting the Holy Land over Christmas. He is particularly touched by the verse "Yet in the dark night shineth the everlasting light/The hopes and fears of all the years are met in thee tonight."

The sentiment of this verse, and all that he and his people have endured the last several years, overcomes him. With no embarrassment, this proud man brushes away the tears. By now I have learned that he is capable of great emotions and unafraid to express them.

Churchill

In the late afternoon, the British and American chiefs of staff meet once again. At this session General Marshall begins to assert himself into the discussions, and he quickly becomes the driving force among the British and American chiefs of staff. Perhaps by coincidence or fate, Marshall was sworn in as chief of staff of the United States Army on the day that Hitler invaded Poland, September 1, 1939.

When he disagrees, Marshall demonstrates that he is bold enough to stand up even to his president and me. He's comfortable in his skin and exudes confidence. He brings to the job "a sterling reputation for honesty, hard work, and integrity." Like Hopkins, he has absolutely no political ambitions, and that endears him to Roosevelt.

At the meeting, Marshall puts a completely new idea on the table. He says it is "his personal view, without any consultation from others," that he feels strongly that the most important consideration before the joint chiefs of staff remains the question of unity of command. He is convinced that there must be one man in command of the entire theater . . . air, ground, and ships. "We cannot manage by cooperation." He submits that such a move as he proposes would solve 90 percent of our troubles.

Although novel, there is no unanimity on Marshall's proposal at the table, and we adjourn for the day. Privately, I believe what he says makes a lot of sense. Essentially, this is the role I cast for myself after becoming prime minister. When war broke out, I also appointed myself minister of defense, in direct charge of running the operational side of the war. No doubt Marshall's idea has merit. The devil will prove itself in the details.

Later in the day, our Christmas dinner in the White House evolves into a state dinner.

Since the Roosevelt's four sons serve in the military far from home, and their daughter remains in Seattle, they include me in their dinner plans along with the prince and princess of Norway, the British ambassador and his wife, and several other British officials. Eleanor and her husband prove marvelous and gracious hosts.

I'll never forget the sumptuous meal they serve consisting of a variety of traditional American dishes. First, we toast to the demise of Hitler as well as the emperor of Japan, using crystal glasses once belonging to Teddy Roosevelt.

Then, we launch into plump oysters, clear soup, turkey, chestnut dressing with giblet gravy, beans and cauliflower, and a sweet potato casserole. For dessert we are spoiled by plum pudding and ice cream, followed by even more of my personal favorite...a liberal serving of fine brandies!

Over the course of dinner I provide the Roosevelts with an update on King George VI and Queen Elizabeth. I know it was Franklin who took the initiative to invite them to come to the U.S. for a visit a little over two and a half years ago (June 1939). They were both nervous and new to their roles following the abdication of King George's older brother King Edward VIII. The latter had been ordained for less than a year before abandoning his throne in order to marry a commoner.

I cannot thank Franklin enough for courageously reaching out to our new king and queen. With Europe on the edge of war, he realized how essential it was to establish better ties between our two democracies. Franklin believed so strongly in the need for cooperation with the British that he assumed the risk of alienating the very strong isolationist and anti-British segments of his electorate. No reigning British monarch had ever placed a shoe on American soil.

Franklin had planned every minute detail of the visit so well, including serving them hot dogs at a picnic at his Hyde Park estate, that they hands down won the sympathy and support of the American people. Speaking of hands, it was most unusual and uncivilized at the time for Royalty to eat with their hands. But, the queen and king graciously played the role to help better reach out to their American cousins.

I observe that the former King Edward must have had some foresight regarding the eventual alliance between Britain and the U.S. He left everything behind to wed the American socialite Wallis Simpson. Quite a scandal I may add! So, I submit to Franklin that the abdication of Edward to marry Simpson exhibits but another example of our two countries' fondness to forge a more perfect union with one another! This brings a course of loud laughter and applause at the dinner table.

Roosevelt

It has been a full Christmas Day in the White House, and who knows how many will follow under the cloud of World War II?

Expressing his appreciation for another fine meal, actually exceptional even by White House standards the last few years, Winston thanks me for not serving him hot dogs for Christmas dinner. Even Eleanor acknowledges how much she had missed a really good meal since putting the White House on a frugal food budget.

Winston says that King George's visit to America boosted his new role as a symbol of the British people. He also thinks that the hot dogs I offered the king and queen at a picnic in Hyde Park helped them connect with the American public.

I ask Winston what progress the king has made with his stuttering. During his visit, I emphasized to the young king that we all had handicaps to work around . . . mine was paralysis from the waist down. I am thrilled to learn from Winston that with some help from a speech therapist, the king has become a very competent and inspirational speaker.

By now Winston and I have adjusted to one another's sleeping habits while under the same roof. I stay up a little later than is my usual practice, and I think Winston pretends to go to bed earlier than he really does.

Churchill

I know that Roosevelt is exhausted from a long day of activity and that Eleanor definitely does not exactly approve of our previous late-night chats. This is Franklin's first Christmas since his mother passed away. Eleanor worries over how he will cope with the holidays. Afterward, she graciously thanks me for helping to lighten his evening and calls me a "nice distraction," whatever that means!

After complimenting our host and hostess for such a splendid evening, I politely excuse myself with the comment that an old man like me needs some rest. This brings laughter, as by now my reputation has spread!

I retreat to the Madison Room to send a communiqué to my family, receive my usual round of telegrams from London, and respond to those that require a reply. Before turning out the lights at 2:30 a.m., I smoke my seventh cigar of the day and tweak the message I plan to deliver to Congress tomorrow.

December 26, 1941

Roosevelt

A Secret Service driver, several heavily armed escorts, and a large police brigade meet Winston at the entrance to the White House for his short drive over to the Capitol Building, where he will speak to Congress. Since so many congressmen have gone home for the holidays, I make the decision that Churchill will deliver his speech in the smaller Senate Chamber rather than the larger, traditional House of Representatives.

When I first met Winston at the airport, just a few trusted people knew he was coming to Washington. Then, it was a reasonable risk to drive him over to the White House in the *Queen Elizabeth*, my government-issued Cadillac, without armor. Now the whole world knows we are together in Washington, D.C. It is no longer as safe to travel in this vehicle. An assassination attempt becomes a possibility.

There were two problems in procuring an armored car from Detroit in the few short days since war had been declared on the United States. First, it was physically impossible to build one that fast. Second, U.S. government rules restricted the purchase of any vehicle costing more than $750! Even for a professional bureaucrat like myself, this restriction under the circumstances seemed excessive. It was pretty obvious we weren't going to get an armored car that cheap.

After explaining all this to Winston, I tell him we at first thought we had a temporary solution for his and my future rides to the Capitol Building because of the quick thinking of one of our Secret Service agents. The agent recalled that he thought the federal government already possessed a car that just might suit the bill. It was Al Capone's, which had been sitting in a Treasury Department parking lot ever since it had been seized from the mobster as a result of the IRS' tax evasion claim against him years earlier.

Capone's 1928 Cadillac 341A Town Sedan was an ingenious spectacle. He had a body shop paint it green and black to disguise it to look like Chicago's police cars of the era. Along with a police scanner radio to know where the cops were, he installed a siren and flashing lights to gain priority in heavy traffic. Then the gangster added three thousand pounds of armor to the exterior and finished it off with inch-thick bulletproof windows.

The car would have been perfect and certainly a fun and entertaining solution until we discovered that the Treasury Department, always hungry for funds, let Capone's car go at auction. Of all places, it was shipped to London!

Winston thought it would have been hilarious to ride in a gangster's car. I told him that Capone had served so much time in federal prison, I didn't think Big Al would have objected to us hijacking his vehicle! When he learned where the car was now located, Winston laughed and said maybe his government could commandeer the vehicle for the prime minister's use.

Since Winston has already travelled in one of my two government-owned Cadillacs, the *Queen Elizabeth*, we create a ploy. He rides to the Capitol Building in the other, the *Queen Mary*, shortly after the *Elizabeth* leaves first as a decoy with someone looking like Winston, hunched down in the seat wearing an armored vest.

I know that Winston is anxious about addressing Congress, and I think the details about his transportation might relax him a bit. I elect not to accompany him. This is Churchill's special moment and I do not want to diminish it by drawing any attention to myself. As allies, it is critically important to our relationship that he wins the admiration of Congress. I hold my breath as I listen to the radio.

As he approaches the U.S. Capitol Building, I visualize platoons of uniformed soldiers and police standing at high alert to protect our special guest.

Churchill

Shortly after noon, I enter the crowded Senate Chamber and take my place at a lectern bristling with microphones. Above my head, large, powerful lamps give the normally dim room the brilliance of a Hollywood movie set. Motion picture cameras begin to roll. I deliberately begin my address on a light note:

> The fact that my American forebears have for so many generations played their part in the life of the United States, and that here I am, an Englishman, welcomed in your midst, makes this experience one of the most moving and thrilling in my life, which is already long and has not been entirely uneventful. I wish indeed that my

mother, whose memory I cherish, across the vale of years, could have been here to see this historical moment.

If my father had been an American, and my mother British, instead of the other way around, I might have gotten here on my own. In that case, this would not have been the first time you would have heard my voice.

Now, I get serious:

For the best part of twenty years, the youth of Britain and America have been taught that war was evil, which is true, and that it would never come again, which has been proved false. For the best part of twenty years, the youth of Germany, of Japan and Italy, have been taught that aggressive war is the noblest duty of the citizen and that it should be begun as soon as the necessary weapons and organization have been made. We have performed the duties and tasks of peace. They have plotted and planned for war. This naturally has placed us in Britain, and now places you in the United States, at a disadvantage, which only time, courage, and untiring exertion can correct.

As for the German forces, with proper weapons and proper organization, we can beat the life out of the savage Nazi. These wicked men who have brought evil forces into play must know they will be called to a terrible account.

Many people have been astonished that Japan should in a single day have plunged into war against the United States and the British Empire.

We know that for many years past the policy of Japan has been dominated by secret societies of subalterns and junior officers of the army and navy, who have enforced their will upon successive Japanese cabinets and parliaments by the assassination of any Japanese statesmen who opposed or who did not sufficiently further their aggressive policy. It may be that these societies, dazzled and dizzy with their own schemes of aggression and the prospect of early victories, have forced their country against its better judgment into war. They have certainly embarked upon a very considerable undertaking.

After the outrages they have committed upon us at Pearl

Harbor, in the Pacific Islands, in the Philippines, in Malaya and the Dutch East Indies, they must now know that the stakes for which they have decided to play are mortal.

When we look at the resources of the United States and the British Empire compared to those of Japan, when we remember those of China, which have so long valiantly withstood invasion and tyranny and when also we observe the Russian menace which hangs over Japan, it becomes still more difficult to reconcile Japanese action with prudence or even with sanity.

Grasping the lapels of my suit and squaring my shoulders, I ask this rhetorical question:

What kind of a people do they think we are? Is it possible that they do not realize that we shall never cease to persevere against them until they have been taught a lesson which they and the world will never forget?

I then express this final thought:

Members of the Senate and members of the House of Representatives, here we are together, facing a group of mighty foes who seek our ruin. Here we are together, defending all that free men hold dear. Twice in a single generation the catastrophe of world war has fallen upon us. Twice in our lifetime has the long arm of fate reached out across the oceans to bring the United States into the forefront of the battle. We now owe it to ourselves, to our children, to tormented mankind, to make sure that these catastrophes do not engulf us for the third time.

Roosevelt

Churchill's address to Congress moves me deeply. He delivers it with a rare combination, unique to him, of emotion, passion, and showmanship. According to the radio announcers, he enters the room wearing a bold, polka-dotted, blue and white bow tie. As he rises to the podium, he grins, puts on his gold-rimmed spectacles, blinks back a few glistening tears that sometimes come to his eyes during such dramatic occasions, and begins his powerful address.

At the conclusion of his thirty-minute address, he flashes a "V" for victory sign and then sits down.

For a moment there is complete silence followed by complete pandemonium. Senators, representatives, Supreme Court justices, and Cabinet secretaries applaud, wave, and cheer. Winston clearly connects with them and many exchange "V" signs with him. His cherubic forehead reflecting in the lights of cameras, Churchill's apple-cheeked face beams. He has clearly won his audience's heart.

The next day, one journalist describes his historic address as "full of bubbling humor, biting denunciation of totalitarian enemies, stern courage—and hard facts."

Churchill

I am thrilled with Congress' response to perhaps the best speech I have ever delivered . . . and none was more important. I hardly slept the night before and continued editing it well into the morning. On the way out of the Capitol Building I tell my bodyguard Walter Thompson that I feel we really hit the target.

But the effort takes its toll on me. I'm exhausted. Ever since I arrived, like all old homes, the White House has been either too cold or too hot in winter. The water boilers that heat all our rooms must have been set on full blast to offset the late December chill in the Capitol. I awake this night perspiring and attempt to open a stubborn window in my room. Suddenly, I feel a sharp pain in my chest that travels down my left arm and I find myself short of breath.

I immediately fear that if I have just suffered a heart attack, it could jeopardize British as well as Allied morale. I summon Sir Charles Wilson, my personal physician and friend who always travels with me.

December 27, 1941

Roosevelt

This morning we learn that Winston fell ill last night. Checking on his progress since seeing him last night, Dr. Wilson invites me to join him in Winston's bedroom as he admonishes him to slow down his pace. With a wink, his doctor looks at me as if I am the culprit responsible for keeping Winston up at all hours of the night. He then advises Winston that he needs more rest than he has been getting since arriving in Washington.

Silently, I chuckle to myself. Clearly both the doctor and I know I wasn't the one lying in bed with remnants of snuffed-out cigars scattered in ashtrays about the room and a half bottle of brandy sitting on the table, along with a stack of telegrams.

As he said nothing about Churchill's habits, I believe long ago Wilson realized the futility of reining in Winston's smoking and fondness for brandy and whiskey. Clearly, Winston shows no signs of alcoholic behavior. His mind is always clear and sharp as is his coordination. The heavy cigar consumption and a few drinks throughout the day are more than likely a byproduct of his high energy level . . . without them he might explode under the stress. If Dr. Wilson diagnosed what happened to Winston last evening, he never reveals the cause to him or me. And, I think to myself if Winston did suffer a mild heart attack, Wilson has just made a gutsy call to keep him functional.

Of course, Winston disobeys his doctor's orders to get some rest, as I often do too. As heads of state, there's just too much work to do and so little time to get it done.

Later that morning I meet with Generals Marshall and Arnold and Secretary of War Stimson to assess the progress we are making with the British chiefs of staff. I surprise Marshall with a conversation that I had with Churchill last evening. In our last meeting, Marshall had been left with the impression that Churchill remained dead set against his proposal to establish unity of command, beginning in the Pacific Theater. He is shocked but pleased that Winston now not only buys into the concept but also agrees with Marshall that the appointment should go to Field Marshall Archibald Wavell, the current commander-in-chief of the British forces in the Far East.

I also mention that Lord Beaverbrook, the British minister of supply, met with me privately to register that he believes we have set far too low a goal for America's production of aircraft and other armaments. He also hinted that perhaps we should look at appointing someone in a position similar to his to give things a kick in the pants. But, he was a little more forceful in his speech. All three men think this idea may have a lot of merit.

Midafternoon we reconvene the joint chiefs of staff. Knowing how well his speech yesterday has been received, and wishing to maintain momentum, Churchill pulls himself out of bed eager to join in the discussions and to reaffirm his position from the previous night.

Like the bulldog that he is, he wants to close the deal on making Germany and Italy our first priority. With a perfect sense of theatrics, Churchill lights up a Havana cigar before beginning what he perceives to be a prelude to some hard negotiations. We find it amusing how he deploys the ritual of unwrapping and prepping a cigar to project a sense of authority, calm, and confidence.

Just because he is so loquacious and amusing, Marshall, King, and I let Winston wind up to press his case. Then we feign rudeness, interrupting him midstream and telling him to catch his breath . . . there is new information he needs to hear first. Initially, he seems mystified and even frustrated that we sidetrack him. Then we spring it on him that we're all in agreement. With clear relief on their faces, Winston and his staff seem pleased and astonished to hear so soon following his meeting with Congress that we have made the decision to militarily prioritize first Europe and North Africa. Until now, they are not accustomed to seeing any quick decisions in Washington. We tell them Congress' favorable reaction to Winston's speech cleared all remaining obstacles holding up prioritizing striking back first against the Germans and Italians over the Japanese.

Our leaders concluded that it's the sensible decision since most of our Pacific Fleet has either been badly damaged or sunk at Pearl Harbor. Unfortunately and sadly, until we can rebuild and repair the Pacific Fleet, we remain incapable of providing much support to our beleaguered troops stationed in the Philippines. In the short term we can have more impact on the Nazis.

Also logistically, focusing on Europe and Africa seems quite justified until we can build enough Liberty ships to support the war on two fronts. A merchant ship can only make three or so round-trips per year supplying the Pacific Theater, whereas the same vessel can make a round-trip to Western Europe every two to three weeks.

Winston is also just as delighted to hear that we have set in motion a plan to replace, at his request, the British troops now stationed in

Northern Ireland. Our troops can complete their training there. Four divisions strong, they will confront any possible German invasion of the Irish coast. This measure frees his British troops to fight elsewhere, where they are so desperately needed.

Our afternoon meeting marks the first turning point in our discussions and negotiations. Although significant differences remain, we began to find common ground. This is because the light bulb comes on when we finally decide to organize our service chiefs not as Americans or British but rather by navy with navy, army with army, and air force with air force.

During the evening Churchill and I briefly touch on an idea of also setting up some sort of Supreme War Council to provide high-level orders to the commander-in-chief in the Far East as well as future appointments in other theaters of war. I think Churchill senses that I will insist that if we do create a Supreme Council, it should be headquartered in Washington.

Logically, Washington is physically removed from the war and more central, especially to many portions of Asia, than London. Left unsaid is which allies might serve on the council. Churchill suggests we table this discussion while giving our chiefs of staff more time to work out other issues. I sense that he is not ready to agree on the matter without getting something in return.

By the end of the day, it has been almost three weeks since Japan bombed Pearl Harbor. The world is now at war and the Allies are scrambling to retreat in the Philippines, North Africa, Malaya, and the Sulu Archipelago stretch of islands. While the Russians are still successfully pushing the Germans back from Moscow, they are losing ground around Fort Stalin in the Sevastopol region along the Black Sea.

December 28-31, 1941

Churchill

As you ladies who have given birth may agree, men generally do not tolerate pain nearly as well as the fairer sex.

As a result of my encounter with the stubborn White House

window, Dr. Wilson diagnosed my condition as overexertion and then recommended a little bed rest. I vacillate between wanting to be assured that nothing much is wrong with me and pestering him with frequent requests to take my pulse. At a fragile and so important time in our negotiations with the Americans, neither they nor the folks back home need to become frightened about my state of health.

Wilson finally just tells me to stop worrying about my damned heart. After hearing this, I finally calm down and my blood pressure drops. I resolve that whatever might be wrong, if anything, nature will have to wait to take its course because I'm just too busy!

Now that I am in North America, I owe the Canadian Parliament a visit to thank them for their significant contributions of resources . . . man-power, materials, and food. Canadian Prime Minister W. L. Macken-zie King has graciously invited me to come to Ottawa. As steadfast and loyal allies, they declared war on Germany almost immediately after us in September 1939.

Since the beginning of the war, many Canadian soldiers and pilots have given their lives defending the British Empire. And just a couple of weeks ago almost one thousand of them were killed, wounded, or captured in the fall of Hong Kong.

I accept Franklin's generous offer to travel to Ottawa on Sunday, August 28, late in the afternoon on the *Ferdinand Magellan*, the presidential special train. His personal coach is quite luxuriously equipped, containing a presidential suite, two guest rooms, a dining and conference room, and an observation lounge. The lounge has been dressed out in cream-colored woodwork, light brown simulated-leather wall covering, and a rich, plush-looking green carpet. The remaining cars comfortably accommodate plenty of security guards and news reporters. But looks are deceiving.

In a country with a history of assassinating its political leaders, the president's train rolls like an above-ground bunker. The windows are equipped with bulletproof glass, the sides fashioned out of thick armor plate, and the floor poured with reinforced concrete to shield occupants from potential bombs set on the railroad tracks.

Travel by government train imposes fewer restrictions on liquor than U.S. Navy vessels. I dare say Franklin's well-provisioned mobile bar stock contributes to a very mellow and relaxing trip north.

Without fear of German bombers coming out of the dark skies, I marvel at the vastness and beauty of the winter landscape and the bounty of natural resources.

In Britain, most of our great forests have been picked bare over the centuries for the building of ships, furniture, homes, and castles. Sadly, some thirty-seven hundred English oak trees were required to build a single warship in the glory days of our British navy in the 1800s.

I know the strains of the Ottawa meetings will not be heavy. I have already faced more formidable ones in Washington. Now I am quite pleased with the progress our joint chiefs of staff are beginning to make on substantive issues that will ultimately shape the outcome of the war. So, I feel I can be absent for a few days. Plus, I always enjoy the company of Canadians . . . both for their gregarious nature and appreciation of British history, not to mention their whiskey.

With the fabric of our shared culture in the background, I tell the Canadian Parliament:

> In the twentieth century the peoples of the British Empire love peace. We no longer seek the lands or wealth of any country. But, we have not journeyed all the way across the centuries, across the oceans, across the mountains, across the prairies, because we are made of sugar candy.
>
> We shall never descend to the German and Japanese level, but if anybody likes to play rough we can play rough too.

Like a biblical prophet, I then thunder a fateful judgment, knowing full well that the Germans will soon learn of this speech.

> Hitler and his Nazi gang of thugs have sown the wind: let them reap the whirlwind.

Then I shift my tone, recalling when the French contemplated surrender in such a short period of time to Germany. I say:

> I warned the French that Britain would fight on alone whatever they did. Their generals told their French prime minister and his divided cabinet that in three weeks England will have its neck wrung like a chicken!

Next I pause before hurling back this taunt:

Some chicken!

Before I can continue, the Canadians jump to their feet and jubilantly cheer. As the noise lessens, I add:

Some neck!

This creates another uproar, and loud laughter echoes around the room. I am so proud to be standing among our Canadian friends, who like us have paid a dear toll in lives to defend the empire.

At the train station, I tell the Canadian reporters, "Let us all go forward together in all parts of the empire. In all parts of the island. There is not a week, nor a day, nor an hour to lose."

Journeying back to Washington, I celebrate New Year's Eve on the train. As we near Brattleboro, Vermont, I stride to the dining room car, armed with a cigar and a brandy. To the assembled reporters and staff aides I give a toast, silently thanking the Americans for joining forces with us: "Here's to 1942. A year of toil, a year of struggle, a year of peril. But a long step toward victory."

Before retreating to my sleep car, one of my aides hands me a brief telegram from Franklin. He congratulated me on the splendid reception from the Canadian Parliament. Then he said, "As your train gently rocks you to sleep tonight, please be advised that seventy-five of the National Gallery's best works have been secretly crated and are on their way to a more secure sight in the mountains of North Carolina. We will take similar steps at other prominent museums across the country to protect our national treasures from the threat of enemy air raids. Thank you Dear Friend for your warning and council on the matter a few days ago."

I crawl between the sheets reassured that the U.S., the slumbering giant who is finally our principal ally, can move with uncharacteristic swiftness and determination when awakened.

President Roosevelt and King George VI as they drive from
Union Station to the White House, June 8, 1939. *FDR Library
and Museum, Hyde Park, New York*

First Lady Eleanor and FDR carving holiday turkey.
FDR Library and Museum

White House Menu

WASHINGTON, Dec. 24 (AP)—Here is the menu for CHRISTMAS dinner tomorrow at the White House, where Prime Minister Churchill will be the guest of honor:

Oysters on the half-shell with Crackers

Clear Soup with Sherry

Celery, Assorted Olives

Thin Toast

Roast Turkey, Chestnut Dressing, Sausage

Giblet Gravy

Beans

Cauliflower

Casserole of Sweet Potatoes

Cranberry Jelly

Rolls

Grapefruit Salad and Cheese Crescents

Plum Pudding and Hard Sauce

Ice Cream and Cake

Coffee

Salted Nuts and Assorted Bonbons

Winston Churchill in his "siren suit" with Harry Hopkins, his daughter Diana, and Fala, FDR's dog, 1941. *APA*

Cartoon of the Big Two plotting the future of WWII.
Washington Post

Churchill in Quebec. *FDR Library*

Chapter Four

A NEW YEAR OF RESOLUTIONS

January 1, 1942

Roosevelt

While Churchill has been in Ottawa, his war-planning team and mine break through several barriers to progress. They circled back to the brief discussion Churchill and I had about some sort of higher strategy-making body to give guidance to the various commanders in charge of engaging the enemy. They conclude such a body makes good sense and call it the Combined Chiefs of Staff (CCS). This is a huge and monumental decision . . . one that I feel leads us a step closer to victory.

Next they kick around the idea of all the Allies having representation on the CCS. I quickly nix it. I am pretty certain I know where Churchill will stand on the matter. I argue that with so many countries joining us in the war, decisions simply cannot be made democratically or by a show of hands. I assert myself saying: "Since the United States, Great Britain, and Russia currently finance the war and do most of the fighting, we should run the war, make the final decisions, and control the military." For these reasons, even though our other welcomed Allies will spill much blood and make tremendous contributions, the war-planning team accepts the wisdom of not granting others equal weight at the war-planning table.

During Churchill's absence, Lord Beaverbrook hounds me about America's production problems. He contends our goals for tanks, airplanes, antiaircraft guns, trucks, and other armaments are far too low, and that they don't anticipate attrition. He challenges me—no, *demands*—that I find out what prevents us from producing more. He ventures to say that perhaps we need to completely overhaul American management methods and production processes. I would have found this insulting from anyone else but Beaverbrook. As British minister of supply, he has already proved what others thought was impossible.

While I am mulling over what Beaverbrook has said, he calls for a follow-up meeting, stating that he wants to bounce a solution off me. I am initially surprised when he suggests that perhaps I appoint Hopkins in charge of overall U.S. production. My first instinct, perhaps political, is to discard the idea. For years I had refused to create such a powerful position, even though many members of Congress encouraged it. My more liberal views favor labor rather than industrial czars who in my opinion capitalize on labor. I tell him I need more time to weigh his suggestion even though I instinctively know Hopkins really is a natural for such a role.

Both Beaverbrook and I concur that over most of the remainder of the Arcadia Conference between our joint chiefs of staff, the whole issue of production—its scale and allocation—will top the list of most controversial issues. I know when Churchill returns from Ottawa he will push a plan that he proposed earlier to have two production committees: one in London, of course overseen by Beaverbrook, and one in Washington, overseen by someone with the kind of skills that Hopkins possesses.

On New Year's Day, after Churchill's long train ride through the night back to Washington, I can plainly see that he remains exhilarated from his successful trip to Canada but looks absolutely exhausted. Nevertheless, he wants to go to Christ Episcopal Church in Alexandria where George Washington and Robert E. Lee worshipped. Once again he sheds tears when he hears for the first time another song, "The Battle Hymn of the Republic."

On the way back, we make a brief stop at Arlington National Cemetery. He wants to walk through Robert E. Lee's home, which sits at the peak of the bluff of the cemetery overlooking the Potomac, with grand views of the Capitol.

He is a bit confused as to how a cemetery came to be on Lee's family home site. I explain that during the Civil War we confiscated the estate as quickly as we could and then President Lincoln ordered that engineers place a cemetery on the property to assure that Lee would never live there again.

Without missing a beat, he only half-kiddingly suggests that after we defeat the Germans, perhaps we should designate Hitler's home a national zoo . . . a place more suited to beasts!

Winston expresses great intellectual curiosity about the Civil War period in American history. Like a young schoolkid craving newfound knowledge, this sixty-seven-year-old man peppers me with questions about the war and its root causes, which I do my best to answer. Then with a short pause, he makes several notes to himself. Afterward, he speculates that perhaps if he lives long enough he will add the American Civil War episode to his series on the *History of the English-Speaking Peoples*, which he had begun prior to World War II.

We return to the White House after our church excursion with a mutual promise that both of us will stand down as much as possible the rest of the day.

Over dinner consisting of Maine lobster, sea bass, and Gulf Coast shrimp and oysters, Churchill surprises me with a belated Christmas present. He announces that he intends to approve my draft declaration establishing a United Nation of Allied Powers, pledging themselves not to make a separate armistice or peace with the enemies. By design, the Allies who join must further pledge to defend life, liberty, independence, and religious freedom, and to preserve human rights and justice in their own lands as well as in other lands. Churchill comments: "The Declaration cannot by itself win battles, but it sets forth who we are and what we are fighting for."

I am most satisfied and grateful for this gift. I think to myself that perhaps we are setting a foundation for world peace and justice that may live on long after Winston and I are gone. I think it prudent to leave unsaid what it may eventually portend for British imperialism around the world. And, it would be ill-timed of me to raise the ire of the British Bulldog, considering how much I have already badgered him on the matter.

After dinner, Maxim Litvinov, Russia's ambassador, and T. V. Soong, China's ambassador, proceed with Churchill and me to the Oval Office to ceremoniously become the first four to sign the Declaration of the

United Nations. Eleanor and some of her dinner guests join us for the historical occasion. All maintain a respectful silence except for Fala, my little terrier. She lays fast asleep by the side of the desk, snoozing, loudly snoring, and periodically thrashing her paws as if in pursuit of a varmint . . . the way dogs often do when they dream. Laughter breaks out when someone suggests that perhaps she is fantasying nipping at Emperor Hirohito and Chancellor Hitler's heels. In our minds the varmints are definitely Hitler and Hirohito and we hope that this ceremony presages their doom!

January 2-5, 1942

Churchill

At this stage, both Franklin and I feel that the Arcadia Conference has finally begun to meet our expectations and aspirations. Of course he is delighted with the Declaration of the United Nations. Of course I harbor reservations regarding how this institution might evolve. But we have bigger fish to fry in the oceans and can ill afford presently to get too constipated over the language of this fledging organization.

There remains much yet to do. With Franklin and my participation, along with a dozen or so of our senior service officers and cabinet members, we continue to plug away at resolving several sticky issues regarding chain of command, division of resources, and responsibilities. The U.S. knows that Great Britain has essentially depleted its financial resources but not our human capital. We think the Arcadia meetings could run another week or two. Lately they have been extremely well prepared and structured sessions that have been untangling a lot of potentially time-robbing issues and differences of opinion on how best to proceed as allies.

Following my trip to Ottawa, it was my original intention to return to England. But I change my mind, deciding it would be a shame to cut these meetings short just because I am embarrassingly self-conscious of overstaying my welcome in Franklin and Eleanor's home.

They both assure me this is nonsense on my part. And Eleanor and her staff continue to think of everything that can make my stay more agreeable. Thanks to a handy carpenter, the nasty window in my bedroom now actually opens and closes with ease!

I know that I have been a demanding houseguest. When our good friends entertain us, Clemmie, my most fervent critic and darling wife, often points out my excessively overbearing nature! Even now she sends me telegrams asking, "Dear Winnie, are you behaving yourself in The White House?" But, of course!

Roosevelt

No doubt, Eleanor frets, Winston corrupts my work habits and schedules. What wife wouldn't? She observes that since his arrival, I smoke more cigarettes, consume more booze, and stay up much later following dinner, after continuing to work a normal day.

I tell her not to worry "as it was not my side of the family that had a drinking problem." On second thought, I immediately regret saying that to her. She looks injured. Both Eleanor's father and brother were alcoholics and died of the disease. Perhaps she is right that I really am short of sleep to hip-shoot such a biting, castigating remark.

I don't dare tell Eleanor how much joy Winston is to be around, in what is otherwise a rather confined and dull social life. Not only is he a grand dinner guest, which she acknowledges, but also as common and comfortable as a favorite old shoe one never wants to throw away. Despite my original reaction to his long windedness and early biases, I now find Winston a brilliant, worldly, and entertaining conversationalist who spins phrases that you can listen to all night without getting tired. He's been to places that I can only dream about and has had adventures that rival Teddy Roosevelt's . . . perhaps even on a grander scale.

I am particularly fond of Edward Lear's Nonsense Rhymes. Every time I began to quote one, Churchill caps the rhyme before I complete it. For example, I started reciting:

> *There was an Old Man with a beard,*
> *Who said, "It is just as I feared!"*

And then, Churchill added:

> *Two Owls and a Hen, four Larks and a Wren,*
> *Have all built their nests in my beard!*

We have great fun entertaining ourselves with such playful nonsense. It momentarily helps relieve the insufferable pressures from the heartrending global conflicts and human tragedies weighing on our shoulders. We both starve for anything humorous wherever we can find it.

His vast knowledge and recall of literature, limericks, and poetry amaze me. Few men I know possess his intellect.

Eleanor acts flustered but never rude toward Winston. As first lady, she is not accustomed to being completely divorced from high-level strategic discussions on matters pertaining to the nation's survival or its future. She particularly influenced many of the decisions I made to help pull the country out of the Depression. To calm her down, I advise Eleanor not to take it so personally. It's a cultural issue with the British and doesn't mean that I lack trust in her or her personal capabilities and insights.

I suppose it makes matters worse when I explain that Churchill, and the other British gentlemen participating in the Arcadian Conference, are not accustomed to engaging women in discussions pertaining to planning military invasions and the cost they may exact on human lives.

That is somewhat truthful but not entirely. Generally speaking, especially in Britain, public politics remains pretty much a man's world, however influential their women may be on them privately. At this point in our tender discussions with the British, Eleanor's strong social views could marginally distract from our main mission to form a military coalition.

Eleanor bites her tongue. It infuriates her whenever Churchill suggests to me that after the war the British and the Americans need to form an "Anglo-Saxon" alliance to guide the world. She intensely mistrusts Churchill's concept of such an alliance, believing it has too much to do with empire building and too little concern for democracy. Furthermore, she hopes the war's outcome will broaden New Deal social programs and extend them beyond our borders. I know the British aren't ready to hear our progressive views, given they are up to their waist fighting Hitler's alligators and now Japan's.

Eleanor says to me, "I find Winston a loveable, emotional, forceful, and very human leader, but I don't want him to write the peace or carry it out."

The poor woman. From her viewpoint, Churchill has claimed her home, her staff, her office, and now her husband.

Churchill

Both Franklin and I insist that our military chiefs and staffs work out the details of joint cooperation in prosecuting the war. Naturally both sides argue and disagree. Franklin and I make it clear that we only want to be involved in grand strategy. Our posture on the matter creates an atmosphere of teamwork that we both feel will endure throughout the war.

Over the next few days our two teams work intensely through a multitude of issues. These range across how long it might take for the Americans to establish a presence in Europe, how we might assist them in the Pacific Theater, and what other countries might join us as allies in the fight against Germany, Italy, and Japan. Last, but perhaps most importantly, we continue to wrestle with the military leadership structure we will all operate under to coordinate and optimize our collective resources.

I eventually back off my desire to invade North Africa as soon as possible to squelch Germany's expanding occupation there. When our Combined Chiefs of Staff turn their attention to allocation of resources, it becomes painfully apparent that we lack enough ships to both transfer American troops to Ireland and also launch an attack. Furthermore, a North African counter-invasion requires a lot of air support. We simply don't have enough planes, even though I believe we have enough British troops.

Our teams also dwell on the Jewish concentration camps and deliberate what, if anything, we can do to rescue and liberate the prisoners. As frustrating and appalling as these camps are, militarily it looks like our hands will be pretty well tied until we can launch a full-scale invasion of Germany and then push into Eastern Europe, where many are located.

We also lament the possible loss or destruction from our military actions on some of the world's greatest artistic, religious, and cultural treasures housed in churches and museums throughout Europe. This didn't seem to concern Hitler when he firebombed England, but it deeply bothers us.

Pressed for time, we don't come up with a solution to the preservation of the world's cultural and artistic treasures. So, we defer the matter pending the possible creation of a specialized military unit dedicated to identifying locations of these treasures and antiquities and recommending strategies to protect them.

Slowly I gravitate back to my late-night work habits and Roosevelt, despite Eleanor's pleading to conserve his energy, often joins me until well after midnight. We talk about many things, including some aspects of our personal lives.

Roosevelt

Through the course of our time together, we continue to explore and discover how much we share in common. For instance, we both have a love affair with the navy, its famous battles, bigger-than-life personas, and fascinating traditions. I tell him that my favorite U.S. Navy hero is Captain John Paul Jones for his role in the American Revolution. His is British Flag Officer and Vice Admiral Horatio Nelson for his role in the Napoleonic Wars.

We share many stories including a few ribald sailor tales not for mixed company. As a measure of his wedding to the institution, Winston rolls up his sleeve and shows me a tattoo of a navy anchor on his right forearm.

With an impish gleam in his eye, he then proceeds to tell me a story about the retired, elderly British Navy officer who puts on his uniform one last time and heads to the dock for one final fling.

The old scoundrel engages a lady of the evening and, after several drinks, takes her up to a room. He's soon going at it as well as he can for a man of his age but asks "How am I doing sweetheart?" for some reassurance. She replies, "Well, old sailor, you're doing about four knots." "Four knots?" he asks. "What's that supposed to mean?" She replies, "You're not sober, you're not hard, you're not in, and you're not getting your money back!"

This brings a roar of laughter from both of us. I've learned that no one enjoys his own jokes as much as Winston.

I ask him how in dealing with a liberal government, so focused on addressing the welfare of so much human suffering during the

Depression years, he managed to secure any resources to help preserve Britain's naval reputation.

Churchill

"Franklin, all my life I have loved the navy and excelled in the institution. In my younger years, I tried both flying and driving. Damned bad at either one! Numerable, but minor, self-inflicted accidents convinced me that I belonged at sea.

"For centuries we British dominated the oceans. The strength of our naval power made us a force to be reckoned with and defended our shores. But not everyone in the British Parliament was similarly anchored in the view that a modern navy was still as necessary as ever, given the rapid evolution of airplanes. Not even cabinet members in my own party.

"The reforms I made to the navy cost money . . . reforms that would subtract from appropriations that the Liberal Party planned to spend on welfare projects during the Depression.

"I remember Lloyd George, the champion of these reforms, scolding me. He said, 'Winston, you've become a water creature. You think we all live at sea. All your thoughts are devoted to sea life . . . fishes and other aquatic creatures. You forget that most of us live on land.'

"To answer my critics, I gave a speech in Glasgow, the capital of our nation's shipbuilding industry. I said, 'The purpose of British naval power is defensive. We have no thoughts of aggression . . . there is this difference between British naval power and that of Germany. The British Navy is to us a necessity . . . it is for them a luxury. Our naval power . . . is existence to us . . . it is expansion to them.

"So, Franklin, I must say this temporarily silenced those pacifists. But, their temperament and steadfast resistance slowed the pace of rebuilding our fleet while Germany forged ahead to build a modern navy, particularly adept for engaging in submarine warfare. Sadly, we have paid a high price, and not until recently have we truly been able to hold our own against the Germans on the high seas."

Roosevelt

I knew that Winston's father, Lord Randolph Churchill, had been so completely focused on his own political life that he was neglectful in raising his son. His father slowly went mad before passing away from syphilis, the unfortunate death of many a sailor, the year Winston turned twenty-one.

I am therefore curious as to whom he thinks might have played the greatest role in mentoring him.

Unknown to either of us, the answer to that question reveals that we shared a common bond and friendship with a man by the name of Bourke Cockran. Bourke had been an eight-term New York congressman. He was born in Ireland and by coincidence in the same year as Winston's American mother.

Cockran was picked three times to be the keynote speaker at the Democratic National Convention, and had strongly supported my cousin Teddy Roosevelt in the 1904 and 1912 presidential elections. I tell Winston it was Cockran who talked me out of my self-pity after being stricken by polio. He convinced me to return to politics. He died in 1923, and I wish he were alive today to see how his intervention in my and Winston's lives has shaped history.

Churchill

Like Franklin, I am amazed we shared a common friendship with Cockran. I had met him on my way to Cuba in 1895 to cover the war for independence from Spain. My mother, who had been a close acquaintance and distant cousin by marriage, suggested that I stop in route to New York City to meet him. She facilitated the introductions. Years later I learned that they may have been lovers at one time. This didn't terribly surprise me. They always spoke of one another with great admiration.

I tell Franklin my first introduction led to a friendship that lasted almost thirty years.

For me, Cockran became like the father I had always wanted. "He was not only a brilliant politician like my own father, but also a scholar. But unlike my father, he was intimate and engaging. He welcomed me into his inner circle of friends and family and drew me into long, animated discussions about classic literature."

Cockran whetted my appetite for great literature and he inadvertently launched my career into politics. He treated me like an equal, sharing his political philosophies and plans as well as secrets in speech preparation and delivery.

He told me to never clutter an argument with lots of points. He said he was most successful in achieving a desired outcome when he "picked the strongest argument on his side and then concentrated on building and mounting it to conclusion." I have never forgotten his advice, and my memories of him serve me well to this day.

Roosevelt

Once we realize the strongest and most common link in our pasts— that being our mutual respect and admiration for Bourke Cockran—our relationship, understanding, and appreciation of one another soars to an even higher and more informal level.

Later in the evening, Winston asks me my taste in music and what are some of my favorite songs. First, I express my affection for George Gershwin. Back in 1934 I invited him to perform in the White House. At my request he played and sang some pieces from the Broadway musical *Of Thee I Sing*. For its barbed and witty look at American political institutions and workings of American democracy in general, I particularly liked the jocular song "Wintergreen for President." Wintergreen, an awful candidate, had no wife and no platform.

For Gershwin's works such as "Porgy and Bess" and "Rhapsody in Blue," I tell Winston I consider the musician a national treasurer and instigator of modern American music—so much so that when Gershwin fell into a coma and was diagnosed with a brain tumor in 1937, I employed government resources to try to expedite medical aid. Unfortunately, it was too late to save him.

For Winston's listening pleasure and mine, I then put two of my favorite comfort pieces on the record player: "The Yellow Rose of Texas" and "Home on the Range." Out of curiosity, he asks me who the Yellow Rose of Texas was. I explain that she was a beautiful, patriotic, and calculating woman who used her considerable charms to distract General Santa Anna long enough to enable General Sam Houston and his Texas freedom fighters to defeat the Mexican army. Her actions helped Texas gain independence at the Battle of San Jacinto.

This intrigues him and that leads to long talk about the women in our lives who have influenced us the most. Our mothers were strong-willed, progressive, powerful, and very protective of their sons.

Churchill, using a nautical term, describes his wife Clementine as like a rudder and keel in his life that always keeps him from going too far adrift. He had married her when he was thirty-four years old and she twenty-three. He adds that if he died and was reincarnated again as Winston, he would seek her out and marry her all over again. In his words, "She has been the foundation of my existence and a sustaining anchor during all my numerous political storms."

As the pressures and urgency from the war weighed on him, he confesses most recently she admonished him, in a kindly way, for his spouts of dark moodiness and tyrannical behavior around those who reported to him.

And by his admission, she is better at managing their financial affairs. For instance, there were times when she had to constrain him from overspending . . . particularly when it involved his beloved estate Chartwell, or another car purchase.

Under such circumstances, he said he had learned that "as one's fortunes are reduced, one's spirit must expand to fill the void." He did this by becoming not only an accomplished writer but also a painter.

I, of course, am figuratively speaking indebted to Eleanor. Early in our marriage, I committed an indiscretion with an attractive executive assistant. When Eleanor discovered the affair she immediately offered me a divorce, no questions asked, no long litigation over the matter.

My mother, upon hearing this news, collared me. She made it quite clear that if I divorced Eleanor, any inheritance would definitely bypass me and go to Eleanor and the next generation.

Now, I can put the matter in perspective and perhaps even painfully laugh a little about it. I knew my mother didn't really mean what she had said. But, what she did mean is that I would be an absolute fool to divorce a companion like Eleanor who could not only enrich my personal life, complement my budding career like no other, and be the best possible mother to our five children.

I would also be a fool if I didn't admit that Eleanor significantly influenced my political career and policies.

For example, in 1941 she penned a "Memo for the President" on the issue of racial justice for African Americans. She wrote that if we didn't begin to fix serious inequities that she had been lobbying to resolve for many years, our nation would be no better than the Nazis! How's that for bluntness!

So in June 1941, I issued Executive Order 8802, which created the Fair Employment Practices Committee. In my opinion this became the most important federal move in support of the rights of African Americans since Reconstruction. My order stated that the federal government would not hire or refuse to hire any person based on their race, color, creed, or national origin. We banned discriminatory hiring within the federal government and in corporations that received federal contracts.

I think that made Eleanor happy and I received no more memos for at least a few months.

Churchill

From what he shares with me this evening about his wife, I can tell that Franklin and Eleanor are intellectually, socially, and politically interdependent soulmates.

With a laugh, he tells me that Eleanor also possesses a good sense of humor . . . relating the story of the prospects of having a rose being named after her. According to Franklin she was excited and honored, but not particularly pleased, to read the description: "No good in a bed, but works swell against a fence!"

We both chuckle at that one. But, the line gives me pause. I know that the two of them no longer sleep in the same bedroom. Perhaps some aspects of their relationship have grown cold. I also know from my own sources of intelligence that Franklin still discretely maintains contact with Lucy Mercer, his former lover. He is also particularly close to and unusually fond of Daisy Suckley, a distant cousin. I also can't help but notice Franklin harmlessly flirting at a recent dinner party with the clearly attractive and shapely Princess Martha of Sweden, who recently fled Scandinavia ahead of the Nazis' occupation.

No doubt, Franklin enjoys the presence of the ladies. Whether or not he is or was carrying on affairs makes little difference to me or the rest of the world, including the press. As long as his abilities to effectively function remain uncompromised, we all need his considerable talents to fight our common enemies. To relieve stress in an embattled world, my tonics come from Scotch, brandy, and fine cigars. Perhaps his come from other sources.

We both agree that the right women can powerfully influence and shape our lives, bringing out the best in us and downplaying our human frailties. I add, though, that some can drive you mad.

I share with Franklin a couple of stories about Lady Nancy Astor, a prominent British socialite and the first woman elected to Parliament. She had a very sharp tongue with some very progressive ideas—and others that were just simply nonsensical.

Lady Astor did not agree with most of my politics, nor did I agree with hers. We were like oil and water, never mixing well wherever we went. And the worst of it was that she crusaded against almost all forms of alcohol.

Our exchanges were legendary. Out of frustration, I once told her, "Having a woman in Parliament is like having one intrude upon me in the bathroom." To that she retorted, "You're not handsome enough to have such fears."

One night we ended up at the same large dinner party. As I inadvertently stood beside her after making a short dinner toast, she leaned over and whispered in my ear, "If you were my husband I would poison your drink." To that I replied, "If you were my wife, I would drink it!"

However, you should never underestimate a woman. Throughout much of the 1930s Lady Astor remained a pacifist and a bigot. But even she came to her senses, dropping her support of Prime Minister Chamberlain, which set the stage for me to replace him. Even some natural enemies can find common ground.

Franklin gets a kick out of my escapades with Lady Astor. He indicates he knew her and that she also had been a frequent correspondent with Ambassador Kennedy, who initially shared similar friendly views toward Germany.

Turning to a more serious discussion about women, I expressed to Franklin that they, in their own unique way, have and will continue to make as many contributions and sacrifices to win the war as our men.

To the point, I share with him a story about one of my favorite British spies, code named "Willing." In my mind she is already a hero and a legend. "Willing," a stalwart Polish patriot, volunteered to work for British intelligence. She happens to be a phenomenal athlete and former beauty queen, with great persuasive powers. "Willing," in search of enemy intelligence, did not hesitate to leverage her plentiful charms with German officers in defense of her country. Several times she had skied into occupied Poland from neutral Hungary to spread propaganda and transport intelligence to and from the Polish underground resistance. She is also an expert in hand-to-hand combat and use of hand grenades. Recently, she personally helped several Polish pilots escape the country . . . and they now fly for us.

We finish off the evening around midnight with a shot of Johnnie Walker Black Label, my favorite Scotch. Both a bit snookered, I then push Franklin quietly down the hall in his wheelchair to his bedroom door, making sure not to disturb Eleanor sleeping in an adjacent room. I whisper, "Good night, Mr. President . . . it's been an interesting and amusing evening."

January 6-11, 1942

Roosevelt

Winston has not been looking well after two demanding weeks of discussion about who is going to do what to whom as we prosecute the war together. I collaborate with my good friend, Lend Lease Administrator Edward Stettinius, to invite Winston to take a few days off and spend some time in his lovely home in South Florida. We know that Winston has not taken any kind of vacation in over three years and that the sun and a little beach time might do him good.

Plus, I need a break from Winston and so does Harry Hopkins. In fact, when Winston leaves for Florida, Hopkins is so drained that he checks himself into the Washington Naval Hospital for a week of bed rest, a round of blood and plasma transfusions, and vitamin injection treatments to boost his energy. He still insists on smoking, drinking late into the night, and working long hours even though his body is wearing out and his stomach processes little nutrients since his cancer surgery four years ago.

Poor Eleanor also expresses her relief to have a brief reprieve. Bless her, she has been working so very hard to assure that Churchill remains comfortable and well attended to while our guest. But, it still goes against her Quaker roots to assure that at every lunch Winston, as has been his custom for many years, gets served beer, port, and brandy followed by a slightly different routine over dinner.

And, she registers her agitation about the pace both Churchill and I continue to maintain while in one another's company . . . especially the last several days.

Eleanor says she dare not give me any details, but she has it on good authority from Dr. Wilson, Churchill's physician, that some time off for Winston will do him a world of good—or is it do the world good? I am not sure I hear her right, that he may have been sicker than reported. When I query her further, she responds that if I can withhold secrets from her then what is good for the goose is good for the gander. Whatever that means, I drop the topic!

Churchill

I realize that I tax the Roosevelts' hospitality. But I am still not quite ready to leave because our British and American military chiefs are getting down to some very serious business regarding their respective roles on the battlefronts.

Therefore, some brief vacation time—some rest and relaxation—begins to make sense. On board General Marshall's personal aircraft, several of my party and I, along with Secret Service agents, head south to Florida. We land on a small airfield in West Palm Beach. This begins a new adventure for me, and I love adventure.

From there we drive an hour south to West Palm Beach. Along the way, it's refreshing to see many luscious orange orchards and even some tropical plants blooming. We also pass some alligators lazily sunning themselves that I hope keep their distance and have never tasted an Englishman.

The local neighbors are informed that the extra activity at the Stettinius property is in preparation for the visit from a Mr. Loeb, a rather portly English gentleman. Well, I can tell you since I know this man personally, "Mr. Loeb" heads straight to the beach, where he frolics completely naked, as is often the European way.

While merrily splashing along, without a momentary care in the world, someone shouts "shark!" The critter is identified as a bull shark, one of the largest of its species. Normally, but not always, they shy away from swimmers.

One of the Secret Service agents quickly wades into the water, beckoning me to come to shore. Just then, the shark circles back out to sea and I shout, "Look, my large bulk has frightened him away!" So after retreating to shallower waters, I carry on like a hippopotamus, half submerged in a swamp.

If Hitler had been there, I am sure with great gusto he would have shouted, "Winston, go deeper . . . swim further out to sea," thinking I'd make a wonderful snack for the great white sharks whose treacherous personality he so resembles!

While in Florida, I listen intently on the radio to Franklin's annual address on the State of the Union to the joint session of Congress. I know what he will say. Before I left he had rehearsed this speech with his key cabinet and military staff and included me and Lord Beaverbrook in the preview.

His speech is vintage Roosevelt. "No soaring rhetorical heights, no poetic lyrics, just simple talk from the heart."

In a defiant voice, he tells the American people, "The militarists of Berlin and Tokyo started this war. But the massed, angered forces of common humanity will finish it!"

Franklin recites his stunning goals for production of military hardware and troop strength. Immediately Congress stands up and cheers. The figures, he says, "will give the Japanese and Nazis a little idea of just what they accomplished at Pearl Harbor."

He informs his fellow Americans that although the country currently only spends 15 percent on national defense, it will soon soar to more than half the Treasury's national income. To support such a gargantuan budget, he asks Americans to be frugal, embrace higher taxes, and buy, buy, buy bonds.

Toward the end of his address, Franklin reminds his audience that "we are fighting to cleanse the world of ancient ills, ancient evils." He emphasizes that all the members of the newly formed United Nations will fight the war to the bitter end, without compromise. And, he finishes on a high note. "There never has been . . . there never can be . . . successful compromise between good and evil." This remark again brings Congress to its feet, loudly cheering and applauding. Afterward, U.S. Secretary of War Henry Stimson tells Lord Beaverbrook that this was the best speech that he had ever heard Roosevelt give and that it finally buried old, lingering isolationist ideas that existed before December.

For the next several days I bob about in the surf like a "huge, well adjusted, and slightly overfed baby boy," enjoying my champagne, smoking a few cigars at sunset, again at midnight, and devouring roast beef and the freshest of seafood to my heart's content.

One evening Mr. Fields, the White House butler who Roosevelt had sent to Florida to cater to my needs, notices an astonishing pile of empty bottles on my work table. I had been laboring late almost every evening and there was quite a collection. I said to him, "Yes, my man, I need a little more to drink. You see, I have a war to fight and I need fortitude for the battle." Then I tell him, "I have a special favor to ask you. I hope you will come to my defense if someday someone should claim that I am a teetotaler." Fields smiles and assures me that he will defend my honor from any such claims.

Following five days of ultra-relaxing and calming warm baths and a therapeutic nourishing Florida sun and ocean, I know it is time to return to reality.

In my mind, figuratively speaking, London will see very little sunshine of the likes of this over the next several years. I find chilling the prospect of informing the king and Parliament that the worst is yet to come in the European as well as the Pacific theaters of war . . . until our American brothers in arms get up to full strength . . . perhaps not for another twelve to eighteen months.

January 11-13, 1942

Roosevelt

I am quite pleased with the Congress and the American public's reaction to my State of the Union address. Afterward, I meet with the press, telling them that I have presented Congress with the biggest budget in the history of the United States. They find it hard to phantom what a $56 billion war budget in the coming year looks like. I say I understand. To their amusement, I jokingly add, "Very few newspapermen know the difference between a dollar and a dime. But then on the other hand, very few presidents do either."

The first morning Winston returns to the White House from Florida, I propel my wheelchair to his bedroom door to ask him a question. After knocking on the door and announcing myself, he beckons me into his room.

Although already midmorning, I am quite surprised to see him completely naked and leaving a trail of wet footprints on the carpet. He has just emerged from a bath and immodestly paces about the bedroom while dictating to his stenographer, Mr. Patrick Kinna. Shocked, I start to retreat back to the hallway, when Winston says, "Mr. President, don't leave. As you can see I have nothing to hide from you!"

Abruptly finishing dictating, he observes that he rarely sees my cabinet members or me take notes. He wonders why, since he and his staff prolifically take notes to remember and document what was said and meant.

I inform him I routinely discourage my cabinet from taking notes so that they can instead fully concentrate on what is being discussed and also feel free to speak their minds without written incrimination. This has been a long-established practice of mine at all meetings, and I believe it helps generate a more robust exchange of ideas and critique of policies. It also helps prevent unsavory comments from getting into the wrong hands, like the press or a political rival. Although I never say it, my other motive is simply I just don't like to be pinned down by the written word. In his usual witty style, Winston responds that he'll make a note of that!

Winston's stenographer shares with one of my aides that over the years Winston has earned a reputation of not just being tireless in his work, but relentless. He said that his staff felt that to watch Winston compose a speech "made one feel that one is present at the birth of a child, so tense is his expression, so restless his turning from side to side, so curious the noises he emits under his breath. Then out comes some masterful sentence."

Churchill

One afternoon after lunch Franklin agrees to accommodate my request to visit Mt. Vernon. The expansive view of the Potomac River from the front of President George Washington's home excites the eye. Perched high on the bluff, the home, though elegant, is rather modest by the standards of British Royalty. I believe Washington intended that the design of estate contrast with the opulence of princes and kings commonly found throughout Europe at the time.

I stroll the grounds for over an hour trying to absorb the historical significance of the setting. As I do so, I begin to feel my American heritage revealing itself. Franklin, noticing how absorbed I am, inquires jokingly if I am conducting my own private séance with George.

I greatly admire President Washington's profound influence on history. It intrigues me how such a conservative plantation owner became a revolutionary force. Just as stunning is how the war drew out his "inherent qualities of fortitude, resilience, and character" that made him the pivotal man in achieving American independence. There is much to admire and humbly try to emulate as Franklin and I confront our enemies.

I often wonder if Washington had been born in England how his life might have played out. Perhaps he would have led a revolution in England and advanced the cause of democracy much sooner. On second thought, George's rebellious ways probably would have gotten him flogged and hanged.

History has a fickle nature. At one time Washington actually coveted and applied for a commission with the Royal Army. It was denied. Nevertheless, while fighting on behalf of the British Colonies in the seven-year-long French and Indian War, he gained priceless political, military, and leadership skills along with notable recognition in the colonies and abroad. Perhaps if he had obtained the commission, Washington would have remained a Loyalist and the outcome of the American Revolution would taken a different course.

On the trip back to the White House, I ask if we can also drive by the Washington, Jefferson, and Lincoln monuments. In the dark shadow of the forces now jeopardizing our two democracies, I want to further sense and feel the presence of these three great men.

Roosevelt

Over several glasses of whiskey and soda this evening, Winston engages me in a lively discussion on what strengths of character these three great U.S. presidents shared in common. We banter the subject back and forth and agree on the following strengths:

First, we conclude that they were not only politically proficient but also willing to sacrifice their political careers for their strong beliefs.

Second, each was able to rise above personal fears to lead the country.

Third, they had an uncommon ability to select skilled men to help serve their country and to give them the leeway to execute policy.

Fourth, they subordinated self-interests for the good of their constituents.

Last, they had a strong grasp of what shaped history. And more importantly, after learning from it, they shared an ability to visualize the future and steer a course toward it.

At the end of the evening Churchill asks me if I ever dream that someday the nation might dedicate a Franklin Roosevelt memorial? In response to his question, I ask if we win the war, can he conceive that his famous "Bulldog" pose, with rippling jowls, might someday adorn the face of a British Pound note.

We both laugh and agree first things first and that neither of us will live long enough to ever know whether we'll become immortalized or scandalized.

Churchill

Both Franklin and I are quite pleased with the seeds of diplomacy that we have planted since our first meeting off the coast of Newfoundland. We have delegated, guided, nurtured, and divided responsibilities carefully and thoughtfully. Our senior military advisors and diplomats have made tremendous strides in ironing out how we should join forces, including an estimated timetable of when events might play out . . . and contingency plans in case of setbacks.

Roosevelt

The one thing that our military advisors and diplomats continue to make little progress on is how to deal with the atrocities that Hitler keeps committing on the Jewish people. By now we are aware that almost two hundred synagogues in Germany have been turned to rubble. There has been a mass exodus of Jews out of Germany, Italy, Spain, France, and Northern and Eastern Europe. A Palestine state of sorts has been set up to accommodate some of them. And, while the U.S. accepts more Jewish immigrants than any other country, it falls woefully short of what I believe we are capable of doing because of archaic legislation policies in effect that set arbitrary immigration limits. Congress is not listening.

My one great regret on this matter pertains to the voyage in May 1939 of a ship named the *St. Louis* sailing from Hamburg to Cuba with 938 Jewish passengers fleeing from the Third Reich. Cuba refused to admit most of them and then our U.S. Coast Guard turned the rest away when they tried to come here. Most passengers returned to Europe to suffer their fate. Clearly the U.S. failed to show compassion, and the whole episode became a bureaucratic nightmare.

The Great Depression, and the resulting high unemployment during the 1930s, put a severe limit on the number of immigrants we were willing to accept. Also, we already had a long established waiting list of German and Austrian citizens requesting to immigrate, far beyond established quotas.

None of this really justifies our conduct and lack of humanity. Knowing what I know now about the situation and the passengers' destiny, I regret not intervening.

Churchill

I tell Franklin that the French underground resistance, as well as the Netherlands and some of the Scandinavian countries, are doing what they can to help get Jews out of Germany.

We remain frustrated because presently there is no way that we can launch a rescue of Jewish and other prisoners housed in concentration camps. We lack the manpower, weapons, and logistical abilities to launch a major ground attack on mainland Europe, let alone push deep into Germany and Poland where many prisoners are incarcerated.

Although we are both at the point of despair, the atrocities being committed upon European Jews serves to frame the issue of what beasts Hitler and the fascist party have become. It fuels our mutual commitment to eradicate this evil from the earth and to use the banner of freedom of religion as one of the rallying points for such a great moral cause.

Roosevelt

As I look back on it, I am so glad I didn't postpone Winston's coming to Washington so soon after Japan, Germany, and Italy declared war on us. His visit actually jump-started our response to these atrocities and accelerated our actions.

I told Churchill while he was in Florida that I had heard from the leaders of most of our major trade associations, bankers, unions, and key industrialists. He is pleased to hear as am I that union leaders pledged a "no strike" policy, promising to encourage their members to work, work, work in defense of their country.

All parties have guaranteed a commitment day and night to doing whatever it might take to destroy our enemies, including accepting and training women to work on assembly lines. Since there will soon be a severe shortage of young and middle-aged men, they anticipate thousands of Rosy the Riveters working in manufacturing jobs and Mrs. Jones working the fields to feed and support a nation now at war.

On the day prior to Churchill's departure, an issue arises that threatens to unravel much of the joint chiefs of staff's hard work. Although we agreed to create a Combined Chiefs of Staff Committee headquartered in Washington, not London, reporting directly to me and Churchill, we still have not yet resolved how to allocate production among the various fighting forces.

The British chiefs propose that we create two Combined Allocation Committees, one in London reporting to Churchill and the other in Washington reporting to me. Hopkins would head up the one in

Washington and Lord Beaverbrook the one in London. Their thought was that each Allocation Committee would care for the needs of the Allies in their assigned theaters of war. This in effect gives the British direct oversight in Europe and Africa on all materials produced by America, an option Churchill prefers.

Both Secretary of Defense Stimson and General Marshall adamantly oppose this proposal. Marshall exerts his military leadership, as he had throughout the Arcadia Conference, forcefully interjecting that it makes no sense to him to have munitions allocated by politically appointed bodies reporting directly to Roosevelt and Churchill, rather than to the Combined Chiefs of Staff Committee. He asks how can the Combined Chiefs of Staff Committee execute grand strategy with an extra layer placed between them and Roosevelt and Churchill? In his mind it undermines the cherished principle of "unity of command" that the conference worked so hard to achieve.

The issue becomes so heated that Marshall requests a private meeting with me and Hopkins. Behind closed doors, Marshall forcefully tells me that he intends to submit his resignation as U.S. Army chief of staff. Without mincing any words, Marshall insists "neither he nor any other chief of staff can plan and conduct military operations if some other authority, over which he has no control, can refuse to allocate the material required to execute the operation." When I ask Hopkins what he thinks, my political soulmate living in the White House backs Marshall, stating that he neither can assume any responsibility for the Washington Allocations Committee unless it reports, not to me, but to the Combined Chiefs of Staff Committee. Likewise, he insists that the London Allocations Committee must also report to the same authority

This becomes a painful moment for me. If I refuse Marshall's demands, the Arcadia Conference will have the rug pulled out from under it. I will have to find another man to replace General Marshall, who has emerged as our most talented military leader, and turn my back on Hopkins.

Once I think through Marshall's objections, I arrive at his same conclusion that "wartime strategy is dominated by the availability of materials" and that to win this war the Combined Chiefs of Staff Committee must have ultimate authority over its disbursement.

Churchill, realizing that he has accomplished the two most important objectives for which he had come to Washington—to combine and synchronize British fighting forces with the Americans as quickly as possible in Europe and to get the Americans to dramatically expand and expedite production of war materials and troops—accepts my insistence on backing Marshall's and Hopkins' position.

So, here are the high points of what we accomplished during the three-week-long Arcadia Conference in Washington with Winston and his companions:

- The Arcadia Conference created a Combined Chiefs of Staff Committee to hammer out how and when to attack Germany, Italy, and then Japan as well as disburse materials.

- Initially reluctant, Churchill agreed to reduce the role he had played thus far as both prime minister and minister of defense. From this point forward he relinquished the personal and direct control he had over the British armed forces. He and I would periodically give the Combined Chiefs of Staff Committee political direction and then get out of the way to let them convert it into military strategy.

- We set the foundation for the United Nations that established the framework of inter-Allied cooperation for waging the war and the twenty-six countries that would be called allies in combating the Germans and Japanese. Because some are surprising and should be remembered as friends, I am naming them: the U.S., Great Britain, Russia, China, Australia, Belgium, Canada, Costa Rica, Cuba, Czechoslovakia, the Dominican Republic, El Salvador, Greece, Guatemala, Haiti, Honduras, India, Luxembourg, the Netherlands, New Zealand, Nicaragua, Norway, Panama, Poland, South Africa, and Yugoslavia.

- In our Declaration of Solidarity among the allies, we were able to include certain principles, including freedom of religion, which the Soviets' Stalin initially opposed. I reminded their ambassador that "freedom of religion" could also mean "freedom from religion." Their ambassador liked this interpretation and Stalin signed off.

- As for production from the United States, we set an initial goal to manufacture 45,000 Sherman tanks in 1942, then 75,000 in 1943.

- In terms of airplane production, we thought we could do 60,000 in 1942 and then 125,000 the next year.

- Although just starting to seriously make them, we committed to produce 20,000 antiaircraft guns in 1942 and 35,000 in 1943.

- Perhaps the most crucial of all in boosting the flow of materials and arms to England and our other allies, we believed merchant marine construction could go from 6 million tons to 10 million over the same two-year period.

These military armaments are staggering goals—four times the estimated rate of German and Japanese production combined.

After receiving input from our unions, captains of industry, governors, and congressmen, I tell Churchill I feel confident we can perhaps even exceed these targets. This statement puts a big smile on the face of Lord Beaverbrook, who kept goading us for bigger numbers.

Funny, when he first hears of our goals, Germany's propaganda minister, Joseph Goebbels, calls them "insane figures!" He has no clue what we are capable of and, if he had, neither Germany nor Japan might ever have insanely declared war on us.

And, as if to reset the clock toward putting an end to the U.S. Navy's embarrassment in Hawaii, Admiral King's first action as our new Navy chief is to "change the abbreviation for Commander-in-Chief U.S. Navy from CINCUS to COMINCH" because the former had been pronounced just as it was spelled!

January 14, 1942

Churchill

This is my last day in the White House. Even though the Swastika now flies over all of mainland Europe, whose conquered nations are virtually

German provinces, I feel proud of our accomplishments. Britain and the United States are now married after many long months of engagement.

While packing my suitcases, I compliment Mr. Fields, the White House butler, on his superb and very attentive service. I assure him as the result of the ample supply of liquid refreshments he provided me during my stay that we will most certainly depart as the best of friends.

In the evening before leaving, I dine alone with just Franklin and Harry Hopkins. I salute Harry for the pivotal role he played in helping Britain, the U.S., and Russia get to the altar.

Oh, I forgot Fala, Franklin's little Scottie dog. She does her diplomatic thing too at the table: performing various tricks, sniffing our shoes, pleading to have her ears rubbed, begging for beef tidbits, and hoping for an opportunity to lick the gravy bowl.

She also accompanied Winston on our meeting at sea in Newfoundland and quickly won the hearts of sailors onboard both vessels. It must have been her heritage! However, she and I got off on the wrong foot early on when she barked and snarled at me during a cabinet meeting. I gruffly raised my voice, disputing some now-forgotten remark, so she paid me back in kind. To laughter in the room, Fala was evicted with a sense of injustice. Several bribes later, we have since become pals.

There are a few important things I want to say before departing.

First, I say to Franklin that you have heard stories about my drinking, some from me, and may hear more in the future. Even Hitler assumes that I am an incompetent drunkard, which I would just as soon he continues to believe. I want him to underestimate me. But, I do not want you to be concerned. You have been around me long enough these last three weeks to know that I do not let my most enjoyable habit impair my responsibilities and obligations. "I believe that I have taken more out of alcohol than it has taken out of me."

I confess that I did develop a great capacity for the beverage after developing a tolerance, and then a fondness, for the substance while living in India, South Africa, and Cuba. Water in those countries was not safe to drink. So we disinfected it, as was the custom, with a splash of whiskey . . . all day long. And when we could, we first boiled it. Even now I don't like a strong drink and just put a hint of Scotch in my soda. I call it my mouthwash.

Then I turn to more serious matters. I acknowledge how difficult it must have been for Franklin to see so many lives snuffed out so quickly and tragically at Pearl Harbor. Athough it's something you never get used to, I tell him what I think in his heart he may already know. Sadly for his country, this just begins the blood that will be shed for freedom.

I encourage him to maintain a steely resolve. He must fortify himself to preserve his tremendous and unique leadership skills to help his people through the suffering and the healing that will come from a "hell on earth experience" . . . an experience that most of his innocent citizens and young soldiers can yet hardly imagine.

Confiding our trust in our new American colleagues in arms, I also reveal to Franklin that we have cracked the Nazis' Enigma Code. I ask him to inform his top command and to keep this intelligence very secret since it gives us, as Allies, a tremendous strategic advantage to anticipate where Germany might attack next.

Furthermore, I explain we may both have to play "God" with what we do or don't do with the knowledge of Germany's intentions. For example, I mention there might come a time when we knowingly sacrifice troops or citizens, aware that there is little we can do to prevent the attack, or to no longer protect them. And secondly, we may both have to withhold this knowledge for the long game. Bigger victories may be gained that outweigh the short-term costs. Franklin says he understands my meaning.

Then to my surprise, he asks me if that was the case with the devastating November 14, 1940, attack on Coventry in the West Midlands, a major industrial city producing munitions and airplane components. I said it was not and that I am thankful to God that I was never asked to make a judgment call in that incident. But, I add that God will judge the perpetrators of the total destruction of Coventry Cathedral, a place of worship for over nine hundred years, and hold Hitler and his Nazi thugs eternally accountable!

I also ask Franklin how he enjoyed the film *That Hamilton Woman* that I had presented to him at our meeting off the coast of Newfoundland. He says he found it immensely enjoyable and thought Sir Alexander Korda, the producer, did a splendid job of actually filming it the United States the year before. Unquestionably, it could not have been made in England during wartime.

I then add that there was something else he needs to know about my good friend and British filmmaker but it must remain strictly confidential. To produce *That Hamilton Woman*, Sir Alexander set up a film company headquartered in the Rockefeller Center. The company was just a screen, so to speak. Actually I had asked Sir Alexander not only to make the film but to use it as a ruse while working for MI-6.

The real task I had assigned him was to establish a safe site in New York City for British espionage in the days before America joined the war. I confess that I had asked my closest Jewish friend to perform a most dangerous task. But the resulting windfall was that we had very useful intelligence on German spies who had been operating in the United States. We now will voluntarily share this information with the U.S. government. At first I think Franklin will be angry with my revelation. Instead, he expresses gratitude for Sir Alex's fine work, not only as a famous filmmaker but also as a British spy!

Even if I did write a few lines for the script, now you know the intrigue behind why *That Hamilton Woman* is my all-time favorite movie.

Then, Franklin updates me on their progress in creating an intelligence network since our Lieutenant Commander Ian Fleming visited last May. Fleming helped Colonel "Wild Bill" Donovan write the blueprint for the newly created Office of the Coordinator of Information (COI).

I learn that Franklin has authorized a substantial $100 million budget to begin gathering and evaluating all information and data that may "bear upon national security." Wild Bill will direct and be charged with building this nascent intelligence organization. Not so coincidentally, the COI will also be located in New York City at Rockefeller Center! Franklin says since our two intelligence gathering organizations will be neighbors, and now that everything seems out in the open between our two governments, he expects plenty of information to be shared for mutual benefit. I chuckle at his remark and say, "Mr. President, I couldn't agree with you more."

We discuss the collapse of France and the Vichy regime—the token French government that the Germans installed to replace the Republic. Both of us despise the regime and view it as nothing more than a puppet state. We also have some doubts that France can ever be resurrected as an important country, given the series of dysfunctional and ineffective governments since World War I.

We do agree to give our full support to General Charles de Gaulle, the head of the French resistance. The Vichy government has condemned de Gaulle to death upon capture. Even though he is arrogant and difficult to work with, we agree to do our best to prevent his capture and execution.

Lastly, I implore caution working with Joseph Stalin. Neither of us have yet met the man, but his reputation as a despot precedes him. As much as I detest communism, I support coming to the aid of the Soviet Union to prevent them from being overrun by the Nazis.

I harbor a very uneasy feeling about the man, almost a premonition, that once the Allies win the war, Stalin might make a massive land grab, subjecting millions more people to the worst that communism offers.

I strongly register with Franklin that we must never totally trust this man. Do you remember when the Soviets signed a nonaggression pact with the Nazis, allowing them to swallow Poland as long as they stopped there? It stunned the world. This man has straddled both sides of the fence. The key to dealing with the Russians rests in our ability to second-guess Stalin and the Soviets' strategic interests.

We both agree that we are masters of our fate. Together we will be doing the noblest of work in the world, not only defending our homes and families but also defending the cause of freedom, whether deliverance will come next year or five years hence.

Ironically, and almost simultaneously, we recite the words of the psalmist: "He shall not be afraid of evil tidings. His heart is fixed, trusting in the Lord."

Roosevelt

Winston's scheduled departure following dinner is 8:45 p.m., but we linger at the table until almost 9:45, not wanting to say good-bye.

Winston says he hopes to revisit the White House in the future. He asks if he did, could he bring a few of his bodyguards, British Marines, for a tour?

With as straight a face as possible, I roar, "Hell no!" I exclaim that the last time they were here in 1814, 128 years ago, they burned the place. Damn it, you Brits are the reason we call this place the White House! As a result of all that smoke and fire damage, the exterior turned black. Afterward, we had to whitewash her. Of course, once I have my joke, I assure him that they will be most welcome.

I finally say, Winston you need to leave. But, before you do, I want you to know that whatever happens to us going forward, I am so happy I was born and empowered to have shared this century with you. You will always be special to me.

In parting, I wish him God's protection.

Winston thanks me and then pauses, adding: "In defense of my country I am ready to meet my Maker. Whether my Maker is ready to meet me is another matter!"

We then drive him to the station to board a train equipped with special security, waiting to take him to Norfolk, Virginia. Hopkins escorts him to a private siding at 6th Street and puts him into his sleeping car. He also hands Winston a sealed envelope to give to Clementine. I am aware of the contents. It essentially says: "Dear Clementine, you would have been quite proud of your husband on this trip. The Prime Minister has been ever so good natured, has not taken anybody's head off, and partaken of food and drink with his customary vigor. Your friend, Harry."

Afterward, Hopkins goes back to the Navy Hospital and collapses from exhaustion!

The next day Winston boards an American, Boeing-built flying boat named *Berwick* to Bermuda, where he intends to board the HMS *Duke of York* to return to England. I hear later from Hopkins that on the three-hour flight to Bermuda, Winston took the controls of the *Berwick* for twenty or so minutes and made several exhilarating turns. What his passengers thought about that, including the British chief of air staff, has never been spoken or recorded!

The fact that he briefly flew the plane did not surprise me. During one of our late-night chats, Winston confessed "that flying gave him a feeling of tremendous conquest over space."

Winston found the flight quite enjoyable. Upon arriving in Bermuda, employing his considerable charms, he persuaded the captain to fly him onward in a big Boeing Clipper capable of flying at a steady 145 miles per hour at eight thousand feet. It would become an eighteen-hour trip through the next afternoon and night.

Apparently he was very eager to return as fast as possible to his sorely missed family and to report back on the success of his trip to King George VI and Parliament.

The HMS *Duke of York* was left to bring the rest of his staff and heavy baggage back to England.

On the trip over the Atlantic, I learned, the pilot became disoriented. He could not identify the English coastline. "The pilot made a snap decision to turn the plane around. Had he not, they would have drifted over Brest, France, and the pride of the German fleet moored in a harbor . . . well protected by hundreds of German antiaircraft guns."

As it turned out, the captain's judgment to change directions proved correct. However, the lone Boeing aircraft appeared to British "radar operators as the track of a lone German bomber headed for England from Brest. Six Hurricanes were scrambled with orders to shoot down the intruder." Thankfully, the Hurricanes never located their target; otherwise, history might have taken another twisted turn.

So, "Churchill arrives safely home, the first head of any nation to undertake a transoceanic flight." And I return to Eleanor's Spartan White House menus and an earlier bedtime.

Winston's three weeks inhabiting the White House just marked the early beginnings of our time together. Over the course of the war, we spent almost 135 days in one another's company and exchanged seventeen hundred messages.

Of course, we did not always agree on many things. But because such a special working relationship had been forged during Churchill's long visit, we learned to argue freely and even occasionally plot against one another. When necessary, we simply agreed to disagree and get on with it.

However, Eleanor insisted that Winston never sleep again in the White House. She said he was ruinous to my health and that she was "sick and tired of him wandering about upstairs with his pajamas on, more or less." In future visits, she always arranged to put him up in the Blair House.

Thus ended our one and only "Big Sleepover at the White House."

Churchill and FDR at the White House with military commanders. *FDR Library and Museum*

FDR and Churchill at a press conference with commanders. *FDR Library and Museum*

Sisters Evelyn and Lillian Buxkeurple left the farm to keep
World War II airmen flying. They typify the millions of women
who worked on assembly lines to help win the war.
FDR Library and Museum

Poster created by the United States of War showing the flags
of the twenty-six countries that pledged to support the Allied
effort according to the 1942 Declaration of the United Nations.
Illustrator Leslie Ragan

Cartoon depicting FDR and Churchill discussing making Africa
the first major joint military initiative.
National Endowment for the Humanities

Churchill briefly piloted a similar Boeing 314 Flying Boat on his
return flight from the USA to Bermuda in January 1942.
Library of Congress

Epilogue

SHADOWS CAST AFTER
THE BIG SLEEPOVER

Franklin Roosevelt, at age sixty-three, died on April 12, 1945, after having served as president for twelve years, through four elections . . . the longest in our nation's history. His friend and trusted confidant Harry Hopkins, age fifty-five, followed him to the grave nine months later. Both had burned themselves out, sacrificing their health in defense of America.

Hopkins, a son of Sioux City, Iowa, and lost in the annals of history, deserves to be remembered as an amazing figure. He had been key in constructing the New Deal and as an emissary at large who was indispensable to Roosevelt in achieving victory.

Roosevelt not only considered Hopkins a crucial aid but also found him charismatic, funny, articulate, and concise.

Churchill took an immediate liking to him, as did Stalin. In an interview with History News Network's Robin Lindley, author Michael Fullilove noted that "Stalin was deeply impressed that Hopkins, despite his bad health, made a long trip to Moscow to discuss an alliance between Britain, the United States, and Russia. Hopkins was one of the few people Stalin would cross a room to greet. He had real admiration for someone so tough."

When Churchill, Roosevelt, and Stalin were asked whom among them they trusted the most, all of them named Hopkins! Like many prominent people who lost loved ones in the war, sadly Hopkin's eighteen year old son, Stephen was killed in combat on the Marshall Islands in 1944.

As Roosevelt predicted in 1941, Britain would undergo tremendous social change following the war. Churchill lost reelection in 1945, with no disrespect for his wartime leadership. Over the last seven years since the beginning of the war, he had been singularly focused and dedicated to assuring Britain's survival. Consequently, he simply lacked a compelling vision for the future that the citizens could buy into.

At seventy-seven years of age in 1951, Churchill was asked by King George VI to form a new government upon the resignation of Prime Minister Clement Attlee. This time he brought a fresh vision of the future and put great energy into executing it. In addressing the House of Commons, he told them he was "always ready to learn" but that he "no longer always liked being taught" at such a ripe old age. But, learn and lead Churchill did. He guided the nation through a postwar economic quagmire and the threat of communism from abroad.

Winston Churchill died in 1965 at the age of ninety. He survived a number of heart attacks and lived to complete his definitive series of books, *A History of the English-Speaking Peoples*. He twice won a Nobel Prize for literature.

You may recall that Churchill considered writing about the American Civil War and peppered Roosevelt with questions about the period. Indeed, he did write about the Civil War, including it in his book *Great Republic: A History of America*.

You may also remember that Franklin mentioned postponing repairs on the White House due to the Depression years. As a result, the building was drafty and either too hot or too cold. This is the reason that Winston tried to open a stubborn window during the middle of the night and then consequently suffered a heart attack.

Three years after Roosevelt's death, the load-bearing exterior walls and internal wood beams were close to collapsing. President Harry Truman had the White House interior rooms completely dismantled and a new internal load-bearing steel frame constructed inside the walls.

While Eleanor Roosevelt's role in the Big Sleepover is understated, her contributions throughout the war as visiting dignitary were enormous. In the late summer of 1943, she traveled for over a month as Franklin's representative and a Red Cross delegate in the Pacific to seventeen islands in the war zone, plus Hawaii, Australia, and New Zealand. She visited hospitals, military camps, and Red Cross clubs, and by one estimate four hundred thousand troops may have seen her. She maintained a grueling schedule and never surrendered to fatigue.

During her tour she travelled twenty-three thousand miles in rugged conditions, spending more than a hundred hours in the air on a four-engine Liberator bomber equipped as a transporter crowded with troops. She was our nation's first first lady to travel the globe in the air.

In columns she wrote while in the war zone, she shared with the American public back home what it was really like for our troops engaged in daily combat, particularly on Guadalcanal where both sides suffered more than twenty-five thousand causalities. Keenly aware that many of the servicemen she encountered might never return home, she tried to make each visit a personal one, offering to write loved ones back home that she had talked to their sons, brothers, and husbands. "When she chatted with the men she said things mothers say, little things men never think of and couldn't put into words, if they tried," one officer wrote. She was like a mother that many soldiers had not seen for over a year. Area commander Admiral William Halsey initially complained what a nuisance and a distraction it would be having to host and protect a middle-aged civilian woman in the war zone. Ultimately he would retract that statement, saying, "Eleanor accomplished more good than any other person or any group of civilians who passed through my area."

History not only informs and entertains, it instructs!

Why Churchill and Roosevelt didn't aggressively publicize the Nazi atrocities committed against the Jewish people and other minorities remains a mystery. In covering this subject in the play, the author felt like he only waded into the shallow end of the pool.

Maggie Barrett in her article *Roosevelt Neither Villain nor Hero for the Jews* observed that "Accounts of Roosevelt's response to the suffering and slaughter of Jews in Nazi-occupied Europe have painted him either as a scourge or a savior. Either he moved heaven and earth to help the Jews, or he turned a blind eye to their situation and did nothing."

In their book *FDR and the Jews*, America University history professors Richard Breitman and Allan Lichtman contend that these extreme views fail to reveal the nuances of Roosevelt's presidency. For example, Roosevelt was "one of the most private leaders in American history." According to these authors he "wrote no memoirs and precious few revealing letters, notes, or memos." So it is difficult to document his true position on the matter of the Jewish plight leading up to and during World War II. Professor Breitman did uncover one previously unknown document that makes a reference to a conversation in which Roosevelt stated in April 1938 that he would like to help get all Jews out of Europe.

Breitman and Lichtman noted that Roosevelt's father raised him not to be anti-Semitic. His mother and wife worked on behalf of Jewish causes. Rafael Medoff, in his article on "What FDR said about Jews in private" presents a somewhat different view. His research surfaced some private statements Roosevelt had made. In these, Roosevelt indicated he perceived that the Jewish people were "overcrowding" some professions and exerting undue power. Therefore, Roosevelt felt immigrants should be dispersed around the country to avoid problems.

Some people ask why Churchill and Roosevelt didn't bomb the roads and railroads leading up to the extermination camps, particularly Auschwitz. The fact is that it wasn't until around the spring of 1944 that the Allies had made enough military advances to reach these camps. By then, military leaders decided to concentrate forces to defeat the Germans as quickly as possible rather than extend the timetable by going after the camps. By then almost six million exterminations had already occurred, almost half Jews.

Professors Breitman and Lichtman write, "Roosevelt's failings emerge clearly. But so, too, does the fact that Roosevelt did far more to help European Jews than did any other world leader of his time." They continue, "Without Roosevelt's (and for that matter Churchill's) policies and leadership, there may well have been no Jewish communities left in Palestine, no Jewish state, no Israel."

Although other polemics may disagree with the position taken in *FDR and the Jews*, it is clear that both Roosevelt and Churchill focused all their energies into winning the war, and thus put an end to the Holocaust.

In the introduction, the author mentions that Roosevelt's and Churchill's personalities and liberal vs. conservative policies were as likely to clash as get along. A few of these traits appear in the book. But, clearly the two formed a close bond at the beginning of their relationship and needed one another badly to set the stage for winning the war.

Not until the last two years of the war did Churchill and Roosevelt have serious disagreements. It was mostly over the roles the Soviet Union would play in future affairs and the dismantling of colonial empires.

Throughout the war Churchill refused to become the king's first minister to liquidate the British Empire. However, he did concede to events that eventually render the end of the empire. While not particularly open-minded on the subject, he tried to buy time by dragging out discussions with Roosevelt and Hopkins on the notion of allowing India to begin the process of developing its own institutions.

Led by India's charismatic Mahatma Gandhi, Churchill was stunned by Indian Nationalists' demands that Britain establish a timetable to leave India as the price for India's support for the war. Throughout the war, neither Churchill nor Roosevelt could untangle or dismiss the dilemmas of self-determination desired by Asian, African, Eastern European, and Middle East peoples.

During the Teheran Conference in November 1943, Roosevelt, Stalin, and Churchill met to discuss the beginning stages of remapping and repowering Europe when the war ended. Churchill simply didn't trust Stalin's communist intentions and felt Roosevelt was being misled. He said: "I realized for the first time what a small nation we are. There I sat with the great Russian bear on one side of me, with paws outstretched, and on the other the great American buffalo. Between the two sat the little English donkey who was the only one of the three who knew the way home."

The next meeting of the Big Three took place in Yalta in 1945 and further cemented Churchill's views that "beneath our triumphs lie poisonous politics and deadly international rivalries between two emerging super powers." Without yet calling it such, he was instinctively anticipating what we now know as the Cold War. Roosevelt's rapidly declining health compromised his strength to stand up to Stalin's land grab and it disheartened Churchill, who proved prophetic.

The friction between Churchill and Stalin grew to extremes. Stalin asked after Roosevelt died that his body be exhumed, believing that Churchill had poisoned him in a plot to rule the Western world.

The newly created Coordinator of Information agency, headed up by Colonel William Donovan and inspired by British Lieutenant Commander Ian Fleming, played a very instrumental role in winning the war. Under Donovan's visionary leadership, high energy, and courageous judgment, the CIO evolved into what we know today as the Central Intelligence Agency. And, after the war, Ian Fleming went on to write the James Bond stories that we are so familiar with. Certainly, history reveals that Fleming had plenty of firsthand experiences as well as imagination to create Secret Agent 007.

A five-pound note and a dime in your pocket will get you images of both Churchill and Roosevelt. Yes, they ended up on the face of their nation's currencies, as well as monuments and numerous stamps. On May 2, 1997, fifty-two years after Franklin's death, President Bill Clinton dedicated the Franklin Delano Roosevelt Memorial that spreads over seven acres in Washington, D.C.

So, what lessons can be extracted and applied to the twenty-first century from the five years Churchill and Roosevelt collaborated to win WWII?

First the war dramatically changed America's landscape and social fabric. Some fifteen million civilians moved across state lines to work in the defense industry, much of it in Texas, California, and elsewhere in the Sunbelt. Another sixteen million fought in the war. As a result, this mass migration of troops and workers from rural to urban areas set the stage to modernize and make over America.

Not until the war were minorities and women given unprecedented opportunities. The precursor of Civil rights issues began to emerge and the sexual revolution and youth movements took root. Ironically, gays in the military were punitively discharged to San Francisco, helping plant the seeds there for gay rights.

Eleanor gave a strong voice to feminists. During the war, she said now is not the time when women should exercise patience. Perhaps thinking of Amelia Earhart, she famously called female pilots "a weapon waiting to be used."

Since the war, technology has dramatically shortened the time and distances of the impact on the rest of the world from conflicts still festering in Eastern Europe, the Middle East, Asia, and Africa. While Churchill sensed future conflicts as a result of how the U.S., Britain, and Russia redrew former national, religious, and cultural boundaries, neither he nor Roosevelt could anticipate their extent today. The offspring of these conflicts continue to remain in the news. Think of the current and past conflicts in Vietnam, Korea, Afghanistan, Pakistan, India, Iran, Iraq, Libya, Syria, Sudan, Yemen, Cambodia, etc.

The desire for self-determination is a very complex issue. When this desire is misapplied by extremists of particular religious or political views, it still leads to oppression of the fundamental freedoms that we often take for granted in this country. Even in the U.S., there exists today one of the greatest political divides we have seen since WWII, centered on budgets, immigration, education, taxes, health insurance, infrastructure, women's issues, and abortion rights.

How these complex issues get addressed is as dependent as ever on skilled leaders, like Churchill and Roosevelt, who rose above their differences to reach common ground to advance the civility of mankind. The world grows weary of politicians and leaders who impose on others their narrow views and self serving interests.

In contemporary American universities and college classrooms on innovation and commerce, Thomas L. Friedman contends "collaboration is being taught as the best way to do anything big, important, and complex." Unfortunately on both sides of the aisle, many congressmen abhor being labeled "dealmakers," when that is exactly what is called for to strengthen and renew America. Unity of action to serve the "common good" is a thought few people would apply to the 114th Congress, or recent predecessors!

Special interests are being confused with principals and it is sapping our nation's strength. Those leaders who could meet our biggest challenges by arriving at a hybrid of the best ideas from the left and right would best serve our country.

When Ronald Reagan got elected as a Republican president, Tip O'Neill, a powerful democrat and speaker of the House of Representatives, recognized that the people had spoken. He and Reagan found a way to work together, and both compromised to advance the nation's interests.

What would Roosevelt say today about the Super PACs? To what extent do these special interests obscure and even abandon principles that have historically united this country and fueled its prosperity?

Interestingly, while running for reelection in 1936, Roosevelt told voters "government by organized money is just as dangerous as government by organized mobs." Throughout his remaining time in office, he loathed both.

Yet today, we have seen at home and abroad how either of them can paralyze government (organized money) or terrorize society (Venezuela, the Crimea, Afghanistan, Syria, Iraq, Libya, North Korea, Cambodia, and other select countries in Africa and Asia).

Yalta Conference Big Three, February 19, 1945.
FDR Library and Museum

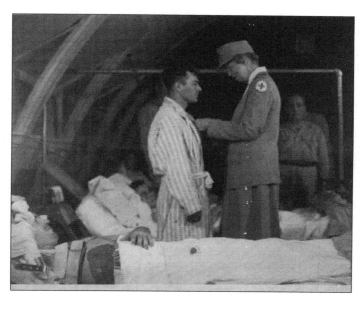

Eleanor Roosevelt in the Pacific Theater, September 1943.
FDR Library and Museum

Franklin Roosevelt Memorial in Washington, D.C.
National Park Service

Palace of Westminster in Parliament Square. *Adam Carr*

BIBLIOGRAPHY/CREDITS

A 2015 search on the Library of Congress website revealed that 762 books have been published on Franklin Roosevelt and 356 on Winston Churchill. Much has been examined, recorded, written, and published!

The following books, articles, and websites were referenced in *Churchill and Roosevelt: The Big Sleepover at the White House* and/or used for inspiration:

Barnhart, Michael A. *Japan Prepares for Total War: The Search for Economic Security, 1919-1941*. Cornell University Press, 1987.

Barrett, Maggie. "Roosevelt Neither Villain nor Hero for the Jews," March 22, 2013. www.american.edu/media/news/20130327_FDR_Jews.cfm.

Bennett, William J. *America: The Last Best Hope, Volume 2*. Thomas Nelson, 2007.

Bercuson, David, and Holger Herwig. *One Christmas in Washington*. The Overlook Press, 2005.

Beschloss, Michael. *Presidential Courage: Brave Leaders and How They Changed America 1789-1989*. Simon & Schuster, 2007.

Black, Conrad. *Franklin Delano Roosevelt: Champion of Freedom*. Public Affairs, 2003.

Bradley, James. *The Imperial Cruise*. Little, Brown and Company, 2009.

Breitman, Richard, and Allan J. Lichtman. *FDR and the Jews*. Belknap Press, 2013.

Brinkley, David. *Washington Goes to War*. Ballantine Books, 1989.

Buell, Thomas B. *Master of Sea Power: A Biography of Fleet Admiral Ernest J. King*. Naval Institute Press, 1980.

Casey, Steven. *Cautious Crusade*. Oxford University Press, 2001.

Christenson, Sig. "A Changing America Marked." *San Antonio Express News*, May 8, 2015.

"Christmas Message 1941." http://www.winstonchurchill.org/resources/speeches/1941-1945-war-leader/christmas-message-1941

"Christmas with Churchill and FDR." The American Spectator. http://spectator.org/articles/38494/christmas-churchill-and-fdr.

Clark, Bruce. "Franklin, my dear . . . : The limits of political friendship." *Washington Monthly*, November 2003.

Churchill, Randolph S. *Winston S. Churchill, Vol. 1 Youth, 1874-1900*. Heinemann, 1966.

Churchill, Winston. *The River War, Volume II*. Longmans, Green and Co., 1899.

"Churchill Addresses Congress," December 26, 1941. United States Senate. www.senate.gov/artandhistory/history/minute/Churchill_Addresses_Congress.htm.

Cochrum, Alan. "Fdr during The War Years: An Enigma Wrapped In a Mystery," A Book Review, *Ft. Worth Star Telegram*, February 9, 2001.

Davidman, Benjamin. "I Believe in the Sun." Holocaust Remembrance, 2006. http://holocaust.hklaw.com/essays/2006/20063A.htm

Davis, Kenneth S. *FDR: The War President, 1940-43: A History*. Random House, 2000.

Dewaters, Diane K. "The World War II Conferences." Presented to the University of Texas at Arlington to fulfill her doctorial of philosophy degree, May 2008.

Domagalski, John J. *Sunk in Kula Gulf: Final Voyage of the U.S.S. Helena*. Potomac Books, 2012.

Dunlop, John. "The Decontrol of Wages and Prices," in *Labor in Postwar America*, ed. Colston E. Warne. Remsen Press, 1949.

Edsel, Robert. *Saving Italy's Treasures: The Race to Rescue a Nation's Treasures from the Nazis*. W.W. Norton, 2013.

Edsel, Robert M., with Bret Witter. *The Monuments Men: Allied Heroes, Nazi Thieves, and the Greatest Treasure Hunt in History*. Center Street Books, 2009.

The Franklin D. Roosevelt Presidential Library and Museum. http://www.fdrlibrary.marist.edu/aboutfdr/royalvisit.html

Friedman, Thomas. "Compromise: Not a 4-Letter Word." *New York Times*, January 4, 2014.

Lindley, Robin. "Fullilove, Michael: FDR: The Greatest Statesman of the Twentieth Century." Interview with History News Network, July 26, 2013. http://historynewsnetwork.org/article/152761

Fullilove, Michael. *Rendezvous with Destiny: How Franklin Roosevelt and Five Extraordinary Men Took America into the War and into the World*. Penguin Press HC, 2013.

Gilbert, Martin. *Churchill: A Life*. Henry Holt and Company, 1991.

Gilbert, Martin. *The Churchill War Papers: The Ever-Widening War, Volume 3, 1941*. W.W. Norton and Company, 2000.

Goodwin, Doris Kearns. *No Ordinary Time: Franklin and Eleanor Roosevelt: The Home Front in World War II*. Simon & Schuster, 1994.

"The Greatest Winston Churchill Quotes, http://jpetrie.my web.uga.edu/bulldog.html

Hamilton, Nigel. *The Mantle of Command: FDR at War, 1941-42*. Houghton Mifflin Harcourt, 2014.

Hamlin, Mrs. Charles. "An Old River Friend." *The New Republic*, April 15, 1946.

Harrington, Daniel F. "The Wonderful Wit of Winston Churchill, Statesman." *Providence Journal*, August 5, 2014.

Hastings, Max. *Winston's War: Churchill 1940-1945*. Alfred A. Knopf, 2010.

Humes, James C. *Churchill: The Prophetic Statesman*. Regnery, 2012.

Humes, James C. *Winston Churchill*. DK Publishing, 2003.

"I Believe," song written by Mark A. Miller.

Jenkins, Roy. *Churchill: A Biography*. Farrar, Straus and Giroux, 2001.

Jones, John Bush. *Our Musicals, Ourselves: A Social History of the American Musical Theatre*. Brandeis University Press, 2003.

Kelly, Jon, and Ian Shoesmith. "The Coventry Blitz 'Conspiracy.'" BBC News, November 12, 2010.

Kimball, Warren F. *Forged in War: Roosevelt, Churchill and the Second World War*. William Morrow and Company, 1997.

Kingsbury, Noel. *The Glory of the Tree: An Illustrated History*. Firefly Books, Ltd, 2014.

Kinzer, Stephen. *The Brothers: John Foster Dulles, Allen Dulles, and Their Secret World War*. St. Martin's Griffin, 2013.

Klein, Maury. *A Call to Arms*. Bloomsbury Press, 2012.

Lindley, Ernst. *The Washington Post*, December 26, 1941.

Lowenstein, Roger. "The Battle Before the Battle," *Wall Street Journal*, July 20-21, 2013.

Lycett, Andrew. *Ian Fleming*. Phoenix, 1996.

Maier, Thomas. "The Secret Boozy Deals of a Kennedy, a Churchill, and a Roosevelt." *Time*, October 21, 2014. time.com/3529756/kennedy-churchill-roosevelt-investment-deal/.

Manchester, William, and Paul Reid. *The Last Lion: Winston Spencer Churchill Alone 1932-1940*. Little, Brown and Company, 1988.

Matthews, Alan. "The Sinking of HMS Prince of Wales and HMS Repulse," 2006. Force 'Z' survivors. http://www.forcez-survivors.org.uk/.

McCullough, David. *In the Dark Streets Shineth: A 1941 Christmas Eve Story.* Shadow Mountain, 2011.

Meacham, Jon. *Franklin and Winston: An Intimate Portrait of an Epic Friendship.* Random House, 2003.

Medoff, Dr. Rafael, Dr. Racelle Weiman, and Dr. Bat-Ami Zucker. "Whitewashing FDR's Holocaust Record: An Analysis of Robert N. Rosen's *Saving the Jews: Franklin D. Roosevelt and the Holocaust,*" September 2006. The David S. Wyman Institute for Holocaust Studies. http://www.washingtonpost.com/wp-srv/style/WhitewashingFDR.pdf

Medoff, Dr. Rafael, "What FDR said about Jews in private," April 7, 2013, http://articles.latimes.com/2013/apr/07/opinion/la-oe-medoff-roosevelt-holocaust-20130407

Middlebrook, Martin, and Patrick Mahoney. *Battleship: The Loss of the Prince of Wales and the Repulse.* Penguin History, 1979.

Middlekauff, Robert. *Washington's Revolution.* Alfred A. Knopf, 2015.

The Monuments Men, film directed by George Clooney, 2014.

Mulley, Clare. *The Spy Who Loved: The Secret Lives of Christine Granville.* St. Martin's Press, 2012.

"Nancy Astor, Viscountess Astor," Wikipedia, www.wikipedia.org/wiki/Nancy_Astor,_Viscountess_Astor.

NPR STAFF. "FDR and The Jews Puts A Presidents Compromise In Context," March 18, 2013, http://www.npr.org/2013/03/18/174125891/fdr-and-the-jews-puts-roosevelts-compromises-in-context

O'Hara, Vincent P. *Struggle for the Middle Sea: The Great Navies at War in the Mediterranean Theater, 1940-1945.* Naval Institute Press, 2009.

Olson, Lynne. Interview by Terry Gross, *Fresh Air,* NPR, March 26, 2013.

Olson, Lynne. *Those Angry Days.* Random House, 2013.

Oshinksy, David. "Congress Disposes ... FDR and the Jews", *The New York Times Sunday Book Review,* April 5, 2013, http://www.nytimes.com/2013/04/07/books/review/fdr-and-the-jews-by-richard-breitman-and-allan-j-lichtman.html

Pearson, John. *The Life of Ian Fleming*. Pan Books, 1967.

Persico, Joseph E. *Franklin & Lucy: President Roosevelt, Mrs. Rutherfurd, and the Other Remarkable Women in His Life*. Random House, 2008.

Peters, Gerhard, and John T. Woodley. "Christmas Eve Message to the Nation," December 24, 1941. The American Presidency Project. http://www.presidency.edu.ucsb.

"President Roosevelt Used to Ride Around in Al Capone's Limousine". The Forgotten History Blog, January 1, 2009. http://forgottenhistoryblog.com/president-roosevelt-used-to-ride-around-in-al-capones-limousine/.

Roll, David. L. *The Hopkins Touch*. Oxford University Press, 2013.

Roosevelt, Eleanor. "Churchill at the White House." *The Atlantic*, March 1965.

Roosevelt, Eleanor. *This I Remember*. Harper and Brothers, 1949.

Rose, Norman. *The Unruly Giant*. The Free Press, 1995.

Roseman, Samuel. *Working with Roosevelt*. Harper and Brothers, 1952.

Rothfield, Anne. "Nazi Looted Art: The Holocaust Records Preservation Project," Parts 1 and 2, Vol. 34, No. 3, Fall 2002. The U.S. National Archives and Records Administration.

Rowley, Hazel. *Franklin and Eleanor: An Extraordinary Marriage*. Farrar, Straus and Giroux, 2010.

Schaap, Jeremy. *Triumph: The Untold Story of Jesse Owens and Hitler's Olympics*. Houghton Mifflin Company, 2007.

Schoenberg, Nara. "*Glory of the Tree* celebrates the under tapped giants among us." *Chicago Tribune*, June 4, 2015.

Seidman, Joel. *American Labor from Defense to Reconversion*. University of Chicago Press, 1953.

Sherwood, Robert. *Roosevelt and Hopkins: An Intimate History*. Grosset & Dunlap, 1948.

Sides, Hampton. *Ghost Soldiers: The Epic Account of World War II's Greatest Rescue Mission.* Anchor Books, May 2002.

Singer, Barry. *Churchill Style: The Art of Being Winston Churchill.* Abrams Image, 2012.

Soames, Mary, ed. *Speaking for Themselves: The Personal Letters of Winston and Clementine Churchill.* Doubleday, 1998.

Srodes, James. *Allen Dulles: Master of Spies.* Regnery, 1999.

"Teaching with Documents Related to Churchill and FDR." www. archives/gov/education/lessons/fdr-churchill.

Truman, Margaret. *Harry S. Truman.* William Morrow and Company, 1973.

"Truman Reconstruction: 1948-1952." The White House Museum. www. whitehousemuseum.org.

"Voyage of the St. Louis." Holocaust Encyclopedia. www.ushmm.org/ wlc/en/article.php?ModuleId=10005267.

"Winston Churchill: Address to the Congress of the United States." Jewish Virtual Library. www.jewishvirtuallibrary.org/jsource/ww2/ churchill122641.html.

Woman in Gold, film directed by Simon Curtis, 2015.

Woolner, David. "Obama v. FDR: Using the Media to Restore Public Trust." Next New Deal, June 16, 2010. http://www.nextnewdeal.net/ obama-v-fdr-using-media-restore-public-trust.

www.names-of-baby.com/browser/a/arcadia.html#.VdKNMlNVhBc

Youngs, J. William T. *Eleanor Roosevelt: A Personal and Public Life.* Little Brown and Co., 1984., http://www.americanrealities.com/eleanor-roosevelt-south-pacific.html

Yuichi, Arima. "The Way to Pearl Harbor: U.S. vs Japan." ICE Case Studies Number 118, December 2003. http://www1.american.edu/ ted/ice/japan-oil.htm.

SOURCE NOTES

Introduction

Roosevelt advocated a liberal viewpoint: Jon Meacham, *Franklin and Winston: An Intimate Portrait*, XVIII.

Both men came from well-respected: Ibid., 12.

She was a glamorous: James C. Humes, *Winston Churchill*, 9-11.

Perhaps because he was so ignored: Franklin and Winston, 13-16.

Unlike Churchill's parents: Ibid.

History views Roosevelt: Ibid., XIX

Astutely aware of their time: David Bercuson and Holger Herwig, *One Christmas in Washington*, 43.

For example, Roosevelt often poised: Ibid.

Similarly staged to affect his British citizens: Franklin and Winston, 144.

Looking ahead, as early as 1941: Max Hastings, *Winston's War: Churchill 1940-1945*, 165.

In contrast . . . Churchill: Ibid.

Chapter One

But, after much of the Western Europe surrendered . . . two big concerns: David L. Roll, *The Hopkins Touch*, ebook, location 1321.

I also learn . . . the first political science course: Ibid., location 214-215.

Even our own ambassador: Winston Churchill, 78.

Our families had been close: Thomas Maier, "The Secret Boozy Deals of a Kennedy, a Churchill, and a Roosevelt," *Time,* October 21, 2014, time.com/3529756/kennedy-churchill-roosevelt-investment-deal/.

Charles Lindberg . . . the unofficial leader and spokesman: Lynne Olson, *Those Angry Days,* XV.

Worse yet . . . Nazi Agents: Lynne Olson, "New York City-A Hot Bed of Spies," Lynne Olson, January 29, 2013, http://lynneolson.com/new-york-city-a-hotbed-of-spies/.

In general, Americans don't believe: Lynne Olson, *Those Angry Days,* XVI.

Plus . . . we lost fifty thousand lives: Ibid., XVII.

Our students in particular voice: Ibid., 223-226.

As if to put an exclamation point: Ibid., XVIII.

To make matters worse: Roger Lowenstein, "The Battle Before the Battle," *Wall Street Journal,* July 20-21, 2013.

So . . . If Hitler Invaded Hell: James C. Humes, *The Prophetic Statesman,* 94.

I ask . . . definition of an appeaser: Maury Klein, *A Call to Arms,* 20.

After his embarrassing defeat: William Manchester and Paul Reid, *The Last Lion: Winston Churchill Alone 1932-1940,* 621.

Of course . . . Germans have accomplished in eleven days: A Call to Arms, 20.

The last night: The Hopkins Touch, location 1499.

My wife enjoys: Ibid., location 1606.

Hopkins has been here: Winston Churchill, 93.

The fact that Willkie: Franklin D. Roosevelt letter to Winston Churchill, January 20, 1941.

In a radio speech: Michael Beschloss, *Presidential Courage: Brave Leaders and How They Changed America 1789-1989*, 194-195.

At Churchill's strong urging: Stephen Kinzer, *The Brothers: John Foster Dulles, Allen Dulles, and Their Secret World War*, 62-64; James Srodes, *Allen Dulles: Master of Spies*, 204-205.

Theoretically, the definition of belligerents: Ibid., 176-178; "Teaching with Documents Related to Churchill and FDR," www.archivew/gov/education/lessons/fdr-churchill.

Hopkins brings us celebratory news: The Hopkins Touch, location 1956.

We both agree that Russia's situation: One Christmas in Washington, 20-21.

When Hopkins leaves for Russia: The Hopkins Touch, location 1993.

After meeting with Stalin: Ibid., location 2321.

Even I, an ardent conservative: Ibid., location 10283.

To fool the press: Warren F. Kimball, *Forged in War: Roosevelt, Churchill and the Second World War*, 97-98.

More importantly . . . replaced thirteen-inch guns: Winston Churchill, 45.

Oddly enough for a navy man: The Prophetic Statesman, 49-52.

Moving from sea to land: Ibid.

We first met in 1918: Franklin and Winston, 109.

To occupy my passage: Barry Singer, *Churchill Style: The Art of Being Winston Churchill*, 168.

And, like myself . . . ends justify the means: One Christmas in Washington, 40.

He is also very brave: Franklin and Winston, 7 and 187.

Like the assassination attempt: Nigel Hamilton, *The Mantle of Command, FDR at War, 1941-42*, 74; Kenneth S. Davis, *FDR: The War President, 1940-43: A History*, 347.

Throughout the campaign: *The Mantle of Command, FDR at War, 1941-42,* 51.

Hopkins says throughout the 1930s: Ibid., 45.

For the most part, the reporters like him: David Brinkley, *Washington Goes to War, 169*; David Woolner, "Obama v. FDR: Using the Media to Restore Public Trust," www.rooseveltinstitute.org.

I also extract one more: Alan Cochrum, "Fdr during The War Years: An Enigma Wrapped In a Mystery," A Book Review, *Ft. Worth Star Telegram*, February 9, 2001

As we approach: Winston Churchill, 95.

Hopkins and I spot Roosevelt: Ibid.

As a token of hospitality: Churchill Style, Churchill, 11.

Tonight, Franklin hosts: One Christmas in Washington, 25.

Upon first greeting Winston: Vincent P. O'Hara, *Struggle for the Middle Sea: The Great Navies at War in the Mediterranean Theater, 17-25.*

When I heard what Churchill: Ibid., 26.

More than my Vice President: Forged in War, 77.

Many of my critics nicknamed: The Hopkins Touch, location 10283.

Churchill is so amazed: Michael Fullilove, "FDR: The Greatest Statesman of the Twentieth Century," Interview with History News Network, July 26, 2013.

However, Winston has his own equivalent: One Christmas in Washington, 104.

He quietly approaches Hopkins: Franklin and Winston, 109.

Just as I feared: One Christmas in Washington, 28.

In contrast: Ibid., 26.

We also ask: Ibid., 27.

I think a joint Sunday morning worship: Forged in War, 98.

Until he can persuade: The Last Lion, 396.

During our return to England: Ibid.

He dresses simply: The Hopkins Touch, location 2173.

With the build . . . Stalin: Ibid.

During his trip: Ibid., location 6871.

Regretfully, at our meeting . . . assurances: The Mantle of Command, 36.

The poem: Benjamin Davidman, "I Believe in the Sun," Holocaust Remembrance, http://holocaust.hklaw.com/essays/2006/20063A.htm

I am particularly proud of the Atlantic Charter: The Mantle of Command, 35-40.

I must admit: "Winston Churchill: Address to the Congress of the United States," Jewish Virtual Library, www.jewishvirtuallibrary.org/jsource/ww2/churchill122641.html.

Perhaps of greater importance: One Christmas in Washington, 33.

Did I mention: Ibid., 3.

Chapter Two

This evening in London: Martin Gilbert, *Churchill A Life*, 711.

On a Sunday that dawned: Forged in War, 120.

With Harriman and Winant by my side: Winston Churchill, 18; *Franklin and Winston*, 130.

Roosevelt says that his cabinet: Conrad Black, *Franklin Delano Roosevelt: Champion of Freedom*, 686; *Winston Churchill*, 97.

My first reaction to the attack: The Mantle of Command, 62.

We were aware that Japan's defiance: Ibid.

As they continue: Michael A. Barnhart, *Japan Prepares for Total War: The Search for Economic Security, 1919-1941*, 144-145; Arima Yuichi, "The

Way to Pearl Harbor: U.S. vs Japan," ICE Case Studies Number 118, December 2003.

As we became increasingly aware of the extent: The Mantle of Command, 65.

Late in the afternoon: Ibid., 65-66.

In the evening: Ibid., 70.

Shortly after midnight: Ibid., 75.

Second, I have a sense: Franklin and Winston, 140.

While I abhor the severe American losses: One Christmas in Washington, 90.

Therefore, it has become urgent: Roy Jenkins, *Churchill: A Biography,* 676.

With all this on my mind: Franklin and Winston, 132-133; *Winston Churchill,* 99.

He presses his position despite . . . losses: Alan Matthews, "The Sinking of HMS Prince of Wales and HMS Repulse," Force 'Z' survivors, http://www.forcez-survivors.org.uk/; Martin Middlebrook and Patrick Mahoney, *Battleship: The Loss of the Prince of Wales and the Repulse,* 234-243 and 330.

Many sailors believe: One Christmas in Washington, 110-111.

I consider Beaverbrook's task: Churchill: A life, 663, 670, 674, and 676

One bright spot . . . Blood and Sand: Martin Gilbert, *The Churchill War Papers: The Ever-Widening War, Volume 3,* 1941, ebook, location 1663.

We also watched: Ibid., 111.

Today I received a wire: Ibid., 116.

During our August meeting: Ibid.

I still have not told Eleanor: Eleanor Roosevelt, *This I Remember,* 240-241.

Instinctively, I reached out: Churchill: A Biography, 671.

That reminds me of the time: Gordon Rayner, "Sir Winston Churchill Quotes," *The Telegraph*, October 13, 2014.

Thanks to Eleanor's efforts: The Mantle of Command, 113.

Well the best way: Eleanor Roosevelt, "Churchill at the White House," *The Atlantic*, March 1965, 1-2.

Seeing that I didn't flinch: Ibid.

So without much thought: Churchill: A Biography, 672.

In the presence: One Christmas in Washington, 126.

With a hint of a tear: Forged in War, 64.

With the loss of thirty-six hundred civilians: Ibid.

An old woman approached: "The Greatest Winston Churchill Quotes, http://jpetrie.my web.uga.edu/bulldog.html; *Winston Churchill*, 86.

I tell Franklin . . . Nazi looting: Anne Rothfield, "Nazi Looted Art: The Holocaust Records Preservation Project," Parts 1 and 2, Vol. 34, No. 3, Fall 2002, The U.S. National Archives and Records Administration; *Woman in Gold*, film directed by Simon Curtis.

Before going to bed: One Christmas in Washington, *127*.

Chapter Three

While most slumber: Churchill: A Biography, 672-673.

On entering . . . map tables: Franklin and Winston, 141.

I ask Harry if . . . met Hitler: Jeremy Schaap, *Triumph: The Untold Story of Jesse Owens and Hitler's Olympics*, 122.

The first one: Winston Churchill, 77.

I was already hearing: The Prophetic Statesman, 123.

On my first full day: Franklin and Winston, 142-143.

On Churchill's first morning . . . postponed repairs: "Truman Reconstruction: 1948-1952," The White House Museum, www.whitehousemuseum.org.

With a twinkle: Winston Churchill, 40.

Franklin particularly likes the story: "Sir Winston Churchill Quotes."

In the afternoon: Washington Goes to War, 184; *One Christmas in Washington*, 140.

One reporter asks: Ernst Lindley, *The Washington Post*, December 26, 1941.

Following our meeting: One Christmas in Washington, 141.

Behind closed doors . . . discuss change: Ibid., 137.

I tell Franklin . . . my chiefs think: Ibid.

Happy hour comes: Franklin and Winston, 144-145.

When Franklin graciously refills: Conversation between Curtis Roosevelt and Alistair Cooke, October 20, 1993, Acct # 95-03, 18, FDR Library.

I had participated . . . Boer War: Ibid., 146-147.

Arcadia is actually: www.names-of-baby.com/browser/a/arcadia.html#. VdKNMlNVhBc

Churchill remembers how vehemently Clemens: Randolph S. Churchill, *Winston S. Churchill, Vol. 1 Youth, 1874-1900*, 542-43.

So Churchill dodges . . . We were wrong to be there: James Bradley, *The Imperial Cruise*, 8.

And it still haunts me: "The Treaty of Portsmouth," U.S. Department of State Office of the Historian, www.history.state.gove/ milestones/1899-1913/portsmouth-treaty.

We are both proud: Biography, Winston Churchill, 25.

When Eleanor challenged: Daniel F. Harrington, "The Wonderful Wit of Winston Churchill, Statesman," *Providence Journal*, August 5, 2014, 1-3

As evidence . . . journalist in the Sudan: Winston Churchill, *The River War*, 248-250.

To placate Franklin: Forged in War, 138-139.

Then with a chuckle: "The Greatest Winston Churchill Quotes."

Clearly Winston draws: One Christmas in Washington, 70.

It is very special: David McCullough, *In the Dark Streets Shineth: A 1941 Christmas Eve Story,* 28-33.

Standing on the balcony: Ibid.

Tonight he introduces: "Christmas Message 1941," http://www.winstonchurchill.org/resources/speeches/1941-1945-war-leader/christmas-message-1941, 147-148.

After the public ceremony: This I Remember, 159.

Later that evening: Winston Churchill, 99

When Hopkins arrives . . . with a zip, Churchill Style: Churchill Style, 172 and Although Winston adores: Winston Churchill,162.

A very nervous nine-year-old: Ibid., 99.

But, Franklin is much more . . . a churchman: "Christmas with Churchill and FDR."

Our first worship together: Forged in War, 9.

I take Winston to the Foundry Methodist: Franklin and Winston, 148.

To my surprise: In the Dark Streets Shineth, 14-15.

In the late afternoon: One Christmas in Washington, 153.

If he disagrees . . . Marshall demonstrates: Ibid.

At the meeting . . . Marshall: Ibid., 163.

Over the Course of Dinner: The Franklin D. Roosevelt Presidential Library and Museum, http://www.fdrlibrary.marist.edu/aboutfdr/royalvisit.html.

Franklin had planned every minute detail: David Levine and Polly Sparling, "Franklin Delano Roosevelt: The Picnic That Won the War, the Royal Visit, the Hot Dog Summit of 1939, and Hyde Park on the Hudson Movie," http://www.hvmag.com/Hudson-Valley-Magazine/December-2012/Franklin-Delano-Roosevelt-The-Picnic-That-Won-the-War-the-Royal-Visit-the-Hot-Dog-Summit-of-1939-and-Hyde-Park-on-the-Hudson-Movie/.

Capone's 1928 Cadillac 341A Town Sedan: "President Roosevelt Used to Ride Around in Al Capone's Limousine," The Forgotten History Blog, January 1, 2009, http://forgottenhistoryblog.com/president-roosevelt-used-to-ride-around-in-al-capones-limousine/.

I deliberately begin my address: Winston Churchill, 100-102; *Franklin and Winston*, 152-154.

For a moment: Ibid.

But the effort takes a toll: Churchill: A Biography, 674.

Later that morning: One Christmas in Washington, 187.

I also mention: Ibid.

Winston is also just: Franklin Delano Roosevelt, 713.

During the evening: One Christmas in Washington, 190.

Since the beginning of the war: The Defense of Hong Kong, www.veterans.gc.ca/eng/remembrance/history/second-world-war/canadians-hong-kong

I accept Franklin's generous offer: "U.S. Car No. 1, National Park Service. nps.gov/nr/travel/presidents/us_car_number_one.html;   *One Christmas in Washington*, 18.

In Britain . . . *Sadly, some thirty-seven hundred English oaks*: Nara Schoenberg, "*Glory of the Tree* celebrates the under tapped giants among us," *Chicago Tribune*, June 4, 2015, 1.

With the fabric: Winston Churchill, 103.

Journeying back to Washington: Ibid.

Before retiring to my sleep car: Robert M. Edsel with Bret Witter, *The Monuments Men*, ebook, location 351.

Chapter Four

Next they kick around: Thomas B. Buel, *Master of Sea Power*, 169.

During Churchill's absence . . . production: The Last Lion, 466.

While I am mulling: Roosevelt and Hopkins, 470.

On New Year's Day: "Christmas with Churchill and FDR."

Over dinner: "A Declaration by the United Nations," *New York Times*, January 3, 1942.

After Dinner . . . Oval Office: Mrs. Charles Hamlin, "An Old River Friend," *The New Republic*, April 15, 1946.

I tell her not to worry: Franklin and Winston, 145.

I am particularly fond: Ibid., 6.

Eleanor acts flustered: Samuel Roseman, *Working with Roosevelt*, 320.

Eleanor bites her tongue: Doris Kearns Goodwin, *No Ordinary Time: Franklin and Eleanor Roosevelt, The Home Front in World War II*, 311.

Eleanor says to me: Ibid.

Both Franklin and I: Forged in War, 99.

Over the next few days our two teams: The Last Lion, 450-53.

I eventually back off: Ibid., 466.

We also lament the possible: The Monuments Men, film directed by George Clooney.

"For centuries we British dominated: Norman Rose, *The Unruly Giant*, 119.

I remember Lloyd George: Ibid.

I said, "The purpose: Ibid., 119-120.

I knew that Winston's: Winston Churchill, 17-18.

Unknown to either of us: Ibid., 24-25.

Like Franklin, I am amazed: Churchill: A Life, 58.

For me, Cockran: Winston Churchill, 17-18.

He told me: Ibid.

Later in the evening: John Bush Jones, *Our Musicals, Ourselves: A Social History of the American Musical Theatre*, 504.

For Winston's listening pleasure: "Favorite Songs," Franklin D. Roosevelt Presidential Library and Museum.

Churchill using a nautical term: Winston Churchill, 37.

And by his admission: Franklin and Winston, 18.

Under such circumstances: Mary Soames, ed., *Speaking for Themselves: The Personal Letters of Winston and Clementine Churchill*, 139.

My mother, upon hearing: Hazel Rowley, *Franklin and Eleanor: An Extraordinary Marriage*, 81-83.

For example, in 1941: "Eleanor Roosevelt, World War II, Fair Employment Practices Commission and African-American Servicemen," http://www.firstladies.org/biographies/firstladies.aspx?biography=33;

Eleanor Roosevelt, "My Day" column, June 18, 1941; Joseph E. Persico, *Franklin and Lucy: President Roosevelt, Mrs. Rutherfurd, and the Other Remarkable Women in His Life*, 325 and 362.

So in June 1941 . . . issued: "President Orders an Even Break for Minorities in Defense Jobs," *New York Times*, June 26, 1941.

Lady Astor did not agree: "Nancy Astor, Viscountess Astor," Wikipedia, www.wikipedia.org/wiki/Nancy_Astor,_Viscountess_Astor.

Our exchanges were legendary: The Greatest Winston Churchill Quotes; *Winston Churchill*, 68.

One night we ended: Ibid.

To the point: Clare Mulley, *The Spy Who Loved: The Secret Lives of Christine Granville*, ebook preface.

Winston has not been looking well: The Last Lion, 462-463.

Plus, I need a break from Winston: Ibid.

Therefore, some brief: Ibid.; Franklin and Winston, 159.

The local neighbors: Ibid.

One of the Secret Service: Ibid.

His speech is vintage: Samuel I. Roseman, *The Public Papers and Addresses of Franklin D. Roosevelt*, vol. 11, 23-24; Roseman, *Working With Roosevelt*, 323-334; *One Christmas in Washington*, 227-228.

He informs his fellow: Ibid.

Toward the end: Ibid.

One evening Mr. Fields: One Christmas in Washington, 236-7.

"After five days: Franklin and Roosevelt, 159.

I am quite pleased: Working With Roosevelt, 20-24; One Christmas in Washington, 228.

The first morning: Winston Churchill, 100.

Although already midmorning: Franklin and Roosevelt, XVIII.

I inform him I routinely discourage: Steven Casey, *Cautious Crusade*, 82.

I greatly admire President Washington's: Robert Middlekauff, *Washington's Revolution*, as reviewed in Jack Schwartz, "The Making of the (First) President," *The Wall Street Journal*, February 21-22, 2015.

History has a fickle: Ibid.

My one great regret: Franklin and Winston, 190.

All parties have guaranteed a commitment: John Dunlop. "The Decontrol of Wages and Prices," in *Labor in Postwar America*, ed. Colston E. Warne, 78-79.

One the day prior: Foreign Relations of the United States: The Conferences at Washington, 1941-42, 192, 198-200; *One Christmas in Washington*, 249.

Both Secretary of Defense: One Christmas in Washington, 250-251.

The issue becomes: Roosevelt and Hopkins, 471-472; *The Hopkins Touch*, location 3082-3087.

Once I think through: One Christmas in Washington, 260-261.

So here are the highpoints: Churchill: A Biography, 675-676.

As for production: A Call to Arms, 293.

Funny, when he first hears: One Christmas in Washington, 230.

First, I say: Winston Churchill, 40.

I confess: Ibid.

Confiding our trust: The Imitation Game, film directed by Morton Tyldum, 2014.

I also ask: Those Angry Days, 367.

To produce: Ibid.

The real task: Ibid.

Then, Franklin updates me on their progress: The Brothers, 63-64; Andrew Lycett, Ian Fleming, 120; John Pearson, The Life of Ian Fleming, 13.

I learn: Ibid.

We discuss the collapse: Franklin Delano Roosevelt, 707-709.

Lastly, I implore: The Last Lion, 444-445.

I finally say: Franklin and Winston, XIX.

Then, we drive him: One Christmas in Washington, 261.

The next day: Franklin Delano Roosevelt, 713.

The fact that: Winston Churchill, 51.

On the trip over . . . The pilot made: Franklin Delano Roosevelt, 713.

As it turned out: Ibid.

Epilogue

Hopkins, a son of Sioux City: The Hopkins Touch, location 50.

Roosevelt considered Hopkins: Robin Lindley. "Fullilove, Michael: FDR:

The Greatest Statesman of the Twentieth Century." Interview with History News Network, July 26, 2013. http://historynewsnetwork. org/article/152761, 1-3.

Churchill took . . . as did Stalin: Ibid.

As Roosevelt predicted . . . social change . . . lost election: The Last Lion, 950-951.

At seventy-seven years of age in 1951 . . . asked by King George VI: Ibid., 1016.

Three years after . . . load-bearing: Margaret Truman, *Harry S. Truman,* 397.

Although Eleanor Roosevelt's: This I Remember, 295-310.

During her tour: J. William T. Youngs, *"Eleanor Roosevelt: A Personal and Public Life;* American Realities, Prologue, The South Pacific," http:// www.americanrealities.com/eleanor-roosevelt-south-pacific.html

In columns she wrote: William F. Halsey Jr., "Teaching Eleanor Roosevelt Glossary," The Eleanor Roosevelt Papers,

www.gwu.edu/~erpapers/teachinger/glossary/halsey-william.cfm; "My Day" column, August 30 and September 2, 13, and 14, 1943.

Maggie Barrett in her article: Maggie Barrett. "Roosevelt: Neither Villain nor Hero for the Jews," March 22, 2013, www.american.edu/media/ news/20130327_FDR_Jews.cfm

In their book: David Oshinksy, "Congress Disposes . . . FDR and the Jews", *The New York Times Sunday Book Review,* April 5, 2013, http:// www.nytimes.com/2013/04/07/books/review/fdr-and-the-jews-by- richard-breitman-and-allan-j-lichtman.html.

Breitman and Lichtman noted: NPR STAFF, "FDR and The Jews Puts A President's Compromises In Context," March 18, 2013, http://www. npr.org/2013/03/18/174125891/fdr-and-the-jews-puts-roosevelts- compromises-in-context

Rafael Medoff, in his article: What FDR said about Jews in private," April 7, 2013. http://articles.latimes.com/2013/apr/07/opinion/la-oe- medoff-roosevelt-holocaust-20130407

Led by India's: Forged in War, 194.

During the Teheran Conference . . . *"I realized for the first time: Franklin and Winston*, 249.

The next meeting . . . *"beneath our triumphs lie poisonous politics: One Christmas in Washington*, 184. Churchill letter to his wife dated May 5, 1945.

The next meeting . . . *in Yalta:* Ibid., 899-900.

The friction . . . *grew to extremes:* As reported by FDR's son Elliott Roosevelt in a *Look Magazine* interview with Stalin in 1946.

The newly created . . . *Donovan: The Brothers*, 60-65 and 88-89.

First the war: Sig Christenson, "A Changing America Marked," *San Antonio Express News*, May 8, 2015.

Eleanor gave: Ibid.

How these complex issues: Thomas Friedman, "Compromise: Not a 4-Letter Word," *New York Times*, January 4, 2014, 1.

Interesting, while running: Presidential Courage, 81.

ABOUT THE AUTHOR

James Mikel Wilson resides in Houston, Texas. He has been happily married for forty-eight years and has a son, daughter-in-law, and two grandchildren. Hopefully the latter, as they grow older, will be inspired by Winston Churchill and Franklin Roosevelt's compassion, faith, resiliency, and sense of the greater good as told in *Churchill and Roosevelt: The Big Sleepover at the White House.* He could not resist writing this book as he begin to imagine the time these two great leaders resided, worked, and forged their union at the White House for almost three weeks during Christmas 1941 to early New Year 1942. This book is a Proud Supporter of Fallen Warriors Memorial (www. fallenwarriorstexas.org) and The National Churchill Museum (www. nationalchurchillmuseum.org).

Jim worked for forty-two years as a sales and marketing manager for Caterpillar Inc. and related companies in North and South America as well as Europe and Africa. His sense of geography and history is incorporated into this book as well as another titled *Paw Tracks Here and Abroad: A Dog's Tale*, Corabella Press, 2014.

Paw Tracks, written for "children of all ages," tells the true adventures of a stray dog who travels the equivalent of almost halfway around the world, escapes four times, and possesses a strong will to survive. In addition to the special bonding that occurs between humans and animals, it teaches some geography, a little history, and the importance of good veterinarian care, nutrition, grooming, and thoughtful kennel boarding. The book is available from most traditional sources.

Snickers, the principal character in the book, shares in first-person voice her marvelous and weirdly true adventures over a twenty-two-year lifespan. *Paw Tracks* is a Proud Supporter of the American Society for the Prevention of Cruelty to Animals' (www.aspca.org) missions related to adoption and animal abuse. The *Peoria Journal Star* and the ASPCA have posted favorable write-ups in their publications.

As a hobby, the author collects books written by U.S. presidents and first ladies.